An
Elephant's
Ballet

It may not be good ballet,
but it's amazing that he does it at all.

An
Elephant's Ballet

*One Man's Successful Struggle
with Sudden Blindness*

ROBERT G. KEMPER

A CROSSROAD BOOK
The Seabury Press • *New York*

To the members of the
First Congregational Church of Western Springs, Illinois,
who loved me three times
when I desperately needed it

1977
The Seabury Press
815 Second Avenue
New York, N.Y. 10017

Printed in the United States of America

Library of Congress Cataloging in Publication Data

Kemper, Robert G   An elephant's ballet.
  "A Crossroad book."
1. Kemper, Robert G. 2. Congregationalists—United States—Biography.
3. Clergy—United States—Biography. 4. Blind—United States—Biography.
I. Title.
BX7260.K38A34   1977   285′.8′0924 [B]   77-22165
ISBN 0-8164-0373-2

Acknowledgments

For me to write a book is an enormous undertaking. As you will learn in the text of this book, I perform literary tasks with great difficulty.

Special appreciation goes to Joan Lichterman, who not only is one of the *dramatis personae* in the unfolding drama but made an encore appearance in the editing of the manuscript, doing what she has done before—turning my "preacher talk" into readable lively English prose.

Eleanor Rounce is more than a secretary, she is my eyes. It was she who typed and corrected my manuscript.

Eddie, Ginny, Betsy, and their mother, Margie, spent many vacation days alone on the beach while Dad was writing on the porch at Tower Hill. They did that without complaint, and I hope they are proud of the result.

Finally, my appreciation goes to the lay leaders of the First Congregational Church of Western Springs, Illinois.

All these are contributors, making this book a collaboration, and I am grateful to each and all.

Contents

WHAT GRACEFUL ELEPHANTS BELIEVE

*An
Elephant's
Ballet*

Prologue

I can read what I have written.

Reading is important to me. I am the editor of a magazine. Two years ago, at the age of thirty-four, Providence smiled on me. The threads in my life had come together in a beautiful pattern.

I had been a voracious reader. I had been an English major in college. I had written free-lance articles for many magazines.

I had prepared for and practiced the parish ministry for ten years. I loved the parish ministry and through two parishes had developed competency in its practice.

Providence has joined this literary and this ministerial strand into one. I am the founding editor of *The Christian Ministry*, a professional journal for parish clergy. There is nothing else I could do for which I am better prepared, nothing that could give me more pleasure and satisfaction. God has prepared me for this moment in my life: I am ready, willing, and able.

My editorial position has meant a change in location. For the first time in my life, I am a homeowner. A piece of turf and a twenty-five-year mortgage are mine (and the bank's) to have and to hold. What is even better, this turf is located in Western Springs, where I had been a ministerial intern ten years before. We are back home among friends.

Margie and I have never been closer. She has grown with me through our changing locations: a teacher who put me through seminary, a pastor's wife, and now the mother of three lovely children. Eddie is six; Ginny, four; and Betsy, one. We look like the all-American family.

Between my work as journalist/minister and the loving, ordered life in our new home I am a happy man. I feel good about everything.

December 1971

I cannot read what I have written.

Something awful has happened! I cannot read. If I cannot read, I cannot edit or write or work. I cannot drive or play tennis. I cannot even play catch with my son.

A strange disease has struck my eyes, first one, then the other. Something has caused the back centers of my eyeballs to hemorrhage. Scar tissue has built up over the hemorrhaging tissue, and it is opaque to light. I have two blind centers. I am not totally blind; I have peripheral vision. But I might as well be.

My little home and family is in jeopardy and disarray. Margie and the children are confused and frightened. My friends at the church are worried for us.

My moods range between despair and anger. What has happened? What have I done to deserve this? O God, what is to become of us?

The doctor said it is "permanent, irreparable, irrevocable." There is no future.

December 1972

I can see what I have written, but with great difficulty.

I have not been fired from my editorial position. The magazine is still being produced, but against great odds.

I have made up my mind to do the best I can. I am being helped by some weird glasses, and, would you believe it, a special television set that reads—sort of. Some wonderful people have helped a lot too. My family has been good to me, and some special people have helped in special ways. I think I can do some things even though legally blind.

Our church wants me to become its minister. I cannot do that. Whoever heard of a blind minister? I know that church: It is large, vigorous, discerning, and demanding. Thank you God, but I am not up to that. It is nice to be asked, but I just couldn't do it.

December 1974

I can read what I have written, but still with difficulty.

I am the senior minister of the First Congregational Church of Western Springs. I preach, teach, and administrate that large, vigorous church. I love my work and it is going very well.

In addition, I am a consulting editor for *The Christian Ministry*. I teach a course in homiletics for Chicago Theological Seminary. There are some things I do not do well; there are some things I do not do at all.

Margie is happy in still another role. She is learning to be the chauffeur for the family, the repairman for the house, and the bookkeeper of the household. It is not the way either of us wants it to be, but we are managing and that will have to do.

Thank you God for saving me.

Those four vignettes are condensed but true depictions of four traumatic years in my life. I am legally blind, and it is not likely that my eyesight will ever improve. But I do see many things. This book is the detailed story of what happened, how I felt about it, and what I learned from it and have come to believe since it happened.

There are many reasons why I wanted to write this book. First, it was therapeutic for me to write it. I needed to remember without passion what I was like and what my life was like in those cruel days. Further, everyone has some cherished dream that may or may not come to pass. I have always wanted to write a book.

Second, I recognize a good story when I hear one, even if it is my own. And a good story is worth telling.

Third, a lot of people have touched my life. This writing is a kind of family reunion. I have brought them together in mind to talk over old times. Alas, they are not all here. I regret the omission of so many who were helpful participants in this story.

Fourth, I want to talk to many people who are like me. There are two kinds of people who are like me. The first are those who are having this book read to them, or are struggling over every word with their own failing eyesight. I want you people to know that I am one of you: I share your disappointment and the agony of your readjustment. But I am also a hope to you: I have learned to live with eyesight that failed. It can be done. The second group like me is everyone else. You and I are people who have lost something precious. In this story it is my eyesight, but it could have been something else or someone else. We all lose something precious to us and do not know how to cope with that. I will not pretend that I know how to do it either, because I do not, but I can tell my story and you can decide if it means anything to you in the living of your story.

Fifth, this is a religious story. It is true I am a minister and true that I am a religious person. But I do not like most religious stories, except those in the Bible. Most religious stories are about "How God and I Made a Million Dollars Selling Real Estate." In that kind of pseudo-religious story God is usually a bit player, a minor character. I do not think or write that way. Personal gods are more like the person than God. I probably could have written a "How God and I Overcame Blindness" story but that is not how I lived it, so that is not how I wrote it. But I am comfortable with religious language. My story had to be told with a strong religious motif because that is how I lived it. I do believe I was saved by God's grace, but you will not find this story peppered with a lot of irrelevant biblical citations. Rather, you will find a man trying to understand what happened to him and how God was involved in the happening.

Sixth, this book may be your only acquaintance with a partially sighted person, and I want you to get a true impression of who we are. We mystify a lot of people. Because we can see some things, we are thought to be a fraud. Because we miss obvious things, we are thought to be stupid or snooty or in a fog. (We may be all those things, but those are not visual defects.) Rather, we live in a twilight, seen/not seen world: We can do some things and not others. It is estimated that there are more than a million of us, so we are not exactly strangers in your midst. It is good for you to know that we are around, and to know who we are and what we need and what we can do.

Those are six good reasons for writing this book, but the seventh is the one that really matters to me. There are some wonderful, beautiful people in the First Congregational Church of Western Springs. As the dedication says, on at least three specific occasions they have done good for me. I want them to know what a wonderful church they are, and how much they mean to me.

Now, before the story begins, I want to explain the title.

A title should be self-explanatory and tell the reader immediately what a book is about. But I insisted that this be called *An Elephant's Ballet*. It is about neither animals nor the dance.

The title is ludicrous. A great, lumbering, clumsy beast cannot do the most demanding of body control movements and disciplines. I laugh at the incongruity of Disney's Dumbo paired with Rudolf Nureyev. As my story unfolds you will see that it is precisely those two dissimilar characters who are struggling within me. It is sad and it is funny.

But the elephant's ballet is more than a comic image. It is part of an observation that was made. I thought I had read the words, but research has not turned up the source. So until the author's lawyer shows up, we will have to assume that the elephant's ballet is an original quote.

I insisted upon the title because it is an idea that became a personal metaphor. "Bob Kemper is like an elephant doing the ballet: It may not be good ballet, but it is amazing he can do it at all." That sets the right tone for this story. In one sense, it's lousy; in another sense, it's amazing. That is how it is with partially sighted people. That is how it is with wounded healers. That is how it is with people who respond to loss. That is how it is with people who are saved by grace.

We may not be good at what we want to be and to do, but really, it is amazing that we do it at all.

HOW A MAN
BECOMES
AN ELEPHANT

The Day
the Lights Dimmed

I remember the day it began.

Great events do not begin with a flourish of trumpets. They begin in ordinary humdrum ways, and we take no note of them at the time. In retrospect we say, "That is where it all started," and, "If I knew then what I know now. . ." That is both the power and impotency of old age. The aged can look back and see clearly the major forces that have been at work in their lives. They know that one must be aware of everything, even the minutest trivia, for it may be a seed that takes root and flourishes in the growing life. The young often ignore the tracings because they are not old enough or experienced enough to believe in patterns, lasting consequences, and the surprising twists of life. The aged are. But unfortunately the aged cannot go back again. They cannot return to the junctions and say, "I should have gone here instead of there." When one takes a turn, by choice or by chance, one can only confront the next turns and not return and reconsider those passed.

In retrospect, what I remember now is the day I first became conscious of a symptom that was to grow in intensity and widen in scope. That may not be the day my disease began; it is the day I became aware of it. Who knows where it really began? It is a mystery, an impenetrable enigma. Was it in the genes of my family history? Maybe, but despite a thorough cleaning of all the skeletons in the family closets none was found with poor eyesight. Was it the residue of some latent time-bomb disease that had been in my body for years? There is such a disease called histoplasmosis, a fungus in the lung endemic to the Mississippi Valley. It is carried by fowls and lies dormant in the lungs until mid-life, when it attacks the cells that support the tissue of the retina. If I was asked once by doctors I was asked a hundred times, "Where were you born, and did you grow up on a farm?" The answer to the first question, "I was born in Alton, Illinois, on the banks of the Mississippi River," invariably brought an "aha, classic case" look to their faces. However, with the answer to the second, "No, I have rarely been at, on, or near chicken farms," their confidence dropped sharply. But the seed of suspicion was planted in me, and for a while I hated all birds. Poor creatures—I wonder if they know doctors are saying bad things behind their wings! Anyway, none of the tests for histoplasmosis proved positive, and the opthalmologist who specializes in the disease, Dr. Alex Krill of the University of Chicago, says it was not that disease. Another blind alley, so to speak.

The reason I did not recognize the great implications of what was happening on the day I discovered the symptoms was that I had no inkling of what to look for. A lump that changes shape, a mole that changes color, even chest pains—these we know are symptoms. But what are the symptoms of eye diseases? Does wearing glasses mean eye problems? No, I never wore glasses in my life. I passed every eye test with flying *As* and *Es*. I did not need glasses to read, drive, or see across the room. So how was I to know my eyes were problem-ridden? Furthermore, glasses are not necessarily indicative of diseased eyes. Usually they indicate a millimeter bend or distortion in the convex lens of the eye. Glasses bend the light back into focus—a bother, not a disease.

There I was, young and not attuned to patterns of change, unaware of precedent causes about to unleash an attack on my eyes, and with no hints or clues—everything perfect. Indeed, the day on which this travail began had been a perfect day. I was doing something I very much liked to do, in a place where I very much liked to be.

I was in the gallery of the United States Senate. I had come to Washington early in the morning to interview Sen. Mark Hatfield (R-Oregon) about the Southeast Asian war. With my trusty tape recorder (an instrument that was to become crucial to me) I conversed with the senator. He was, as always, busy, so the interview was brief, but I had what I needed. My thoughts were on what he had said, and how to incorporate his views into editorial material for *The Christian Century,* the magazine for which I was an associate editor.

Washington, D.C., is an exhilarating city. So deep in our psyches is the power of place that this place of national power lifts the spirit and delights the eye. My plane would not return to Chicago until late afternoon so I had time to wander about. Illinois had recently elected a new senator, Adlai E. Stevenson III. As I had remotely known Adlai E. Stevenson III through our common membership on the board of directors of the Chicago Theological Seminary, I went to his office to see if he had arrived in Washington and to wish him well in his new position.

Senator Stevenson's secretary said he was on the floor of the Senate at that time, but if I wished to speak with him she would arrange a meeting in the cloakroom. What a stroke of good fortune! I had never been in the sequestered outer chamber of the world's greatest deliberative

body. I took the tram underground to the Capitol and
went up to the main floor. A guard barred the door to the
cloakroom. I showed my press credentials and said in a
too-loud voice, "Senator Stevenson is expecting me." The
guard called on the phone and said the senator was on the
floor for a roll call vote, but I could wait for him in the
cloakroom. What a break!

I triumphantly strode into the room. I remember the
scene: massive furniture and fixtures, faces of the well-
publicized all around—the appearance of a lobby in a
wealthy man's club. Senator Stevenson arrived and
pretended to remember me. We chatted for about five
minutes and he had to return to the floor, where for the
first time he was to sit in the chair as president pro tem of
the Senate. He was as excited about that as I was about
being in the cloakroom.

I decided to go upstairs and sit in the gallery that sur-
rounds the chamber of the Senate. I could watch the new
junior senator from Illinois preside over the business of the
one hundred senators of the United States of America. As
usual, there were only about eight persons on the floor,
and the droning voice and dry rhetoric of Wayne Morse
was the only business of the government that day. I
looked at Senator Stevenson in the massive chair usually
occupied by the vice-president of the United States.

But as I looked, I saw two of him.

For the first time, I was seeing double. I blinked my
eyes, shook my head, and looked away and then back. I
was seeing double. I thought, "Boy, am I excited!" Small-
time, small-town, small writer was in the presence of the
"biggies" and was really shook up! I smiled inwardly.
Power does go to your head, I thought.

I left Washington and returned to Chicago, seeing normally in well-lit areas. But when the place was a little

darker than normal, I saw double. I told Margie about the excitement of the day and casually mentioned seeing double in the Senate. She, too, thought it was excitement and we went on to other, more important, things, like the children, the house, and the next trip I was going to make.

My first diagnosis was excitement, but the double vision persisted in underlit areas. My second self-diagnosis was that I was working too hard and reading too much. I resolved to go a little easier—have to pay attention to those old body signals, right? I did not change my pattern much, but still the double vision lurked around dark places. So with a "ha-ha" attitude I said to Margie, "I'll bet I am going to have to start wearing glasses—the first sign of aging" (I was thirty-six). I asked her if we knew an opthalmologist. We were relatively new in Western Springs and had had no occasion to see an eye doctor in the two years we were there. She said she had met a young opthalmologist, Dr. John Hackett, at a free screening for glaucoma held at the local hospital. His was the only name she knew and she said she would make an appointment. She called and casually mentioned the double vision symptom. I got an appointment that week. That should have told me something, but it did not.

Dr. Hackett and I were going to keep steady company for about a year, but I did not know that—or the seriousness of that double vision—when I walked into his office. He did all the perfunctory things: had me read the chart, shined lights in the eye, and took a health history. That health history was boring reading: never hospitalized, never operated on; mumps, measles, chicken pox were the only "yes" answers to that long, frightening list of infirmities and afflictions. "Strong as a horse, eh Doc?" I said. He said nothing, but told me he wanted to dilate my pupils. He warned me it would distort my vision for a few hours, but the routine was necessary to loosen the convex lens so he could better see the inside of my eye. All right, I thought, but I was to drive to a family Christmas gathering that night. My wife did not like to drive in traffic, but just this once I guessed she could manage.

Since that first time my pupils have been dilated scores of times. I never liked it. The drops made my eyes water, and I had to sit in the waiting room crying and watching the world go out of focus. Wow, what a metaphor of what the next year would be for me. Only I did not understand the metaphor. This time, after the dilation, he pulled out of his instrument kit some powerful lights. "Hey, Doc, that's bright! You must be able to see the soles of my feet with that thing—by the way, how is my soul?" Ha. He didn't laugh at my stupid remarks, and told me to come back in a week. "But it's Christmas vacation and I had planned to spend some time with the children." "Come back during that week," he insisted, and I agreed.

I learned later that I was seeing double because not enough light was reaching the retina of one eye to activate the muscles that correct the astigmatism of bifocal vision. The left eye had some diminishment of light stimulation, and that was why I experienced seeing double. Why was the left eye perceiving less light? That was the next question.

'Tis the Season to Be Jolly

Christmas makes me mellow. More accurately, there are moments in the Christmas season that are very emotional, very good, very mellow. I positively loathe and despise the hurly-burly hucksterism of the Christmas season. I hate having to buy presents for people who have everything. I hate the social rat race of open houses, punch bowls, and forced gaiety. I dislike the haggard looks of the shoppers seen on my end-of-day train ride from Chicago. I do not like the ill-mannered, curt, hostile shoppers and clerks. Is this a joyous festival or is this a punishment for materialistic excesses?

But the other side of Christmas is when the clamor ceases momentarily and one is left in the quiet of the night to reflect on this particular moment in one's life. My romantic recollection of this moment is associated with crackling fires in the hearth of one's own home, after church, after the children are in bed and the work for the next morning is done. Then, I sit and think. It is a kind of meditative prayer time.

December 25, 1971, is not a romanticized recollection. That's how it was. I had good reason to be mellow that night: My world was very good. Only an insensitive vegetable does not have a few mellow moments when the livin' is good and 'tis the season to be jolly.

I counted my blessings as they passed through my mellow mood that night.

First, there was Margie. We were both thirty-six, and 1971 was an arithmetical landmark for us: We had known each other for eighteen years. From that year on, more of my life would have been spent with her than without her. "I've grown accustomed to her face," sang Prof. Henry Higgins. My fair lady has a beautiful face. The dominant feature of her face—indeed, of her personality—is her smile. She always smiles, and everyone who sees her smiles back at her. She is pleasant. Sure, her moods go up and down—she is no mannequin. But she is one of the most emotionally stable of women. She is cheery, optimistic, happy. I felt I had always loved that smiling face. It made me glad—and that night, mellow.

In character and life-style Margie accepts most of the conventions of our time and place. She believes a woman's place is in the home. She believes the husband is the provider and the wife keeps the house, pleasing him and helping him where she can. Motherhood is her *raison d'etre.* Some women just seem to transform their own childhood into the childhood of their own children, and that's what Margie does for ours. She believes in God and his goodness—she never had reason to doubt it. She has come herself from a pious and devoted family, and though she is not as methodical in her piety as they were, it lives on in her. Maybe that is what shines through her smile.

She, too, was mellow on that Christmas Eve. She had hassled the exuberance of the children in those weeks, battled the crowds in the stores, labored to decorate the house and table for the festival of Christmas. It was a good moment for her too. We had recently moved into a home of our choosing, always having lived in parsonages. The fireplace crackling before us was a symbol, the hearth representing the light, warmth, quiet, and pleasure of this time of life. She was comfortable with me because she knew I was doing what I wanted to do, and was surrounded by the daily miracles of growing children. She had good friends, neighbors, and the love of her family of origin in nearby Oak Park.

It was a good night for me. There was Margie and the new house and upstairs the children. Twenty miles away, in Chicago, was my office. I was an associate editor of *The Christian Century*, a weekly journal of news and opinion, and founding editor of *The Century*'s companion publication, *The Christian Ministry*.

Editing *Ministry* was desirable to me personally. I had been a reader and writer all my life. I was an editor of my high school newspaper and yearbook, an English major in college, and at the Federated Theological Faculties of the University of Chicago I had majored in religion and art, the theological interpretation of literature. Journalism entailed reading and writing, and my background had steered me to this very timely and appropriate work.

Editing *Ministry* also was highly desirable to me professionally. I was an ordained minister of Christ. My father was a minister, and the genealogy of my family is intertwined with the history of the Congregational Church. "I am a Pilgrim right down to the buckles on my shoes," as Margie says. In my earlier search for a vocation I had resisted the ministry. Should one be so conventional as to follow in one's father's footsteps? Later I came to understand that there are powerful psychological forces related to vocational choice. By personality I am a mediator: I find myself in the middle. I was not captain of the football team but president of the student body. Why? Because my leadership style was to mediate conflict between my peers and school authorities. Even though I went through the battery of tests and the agonies of rationality and rationalization about vocational choice, in a real sense my being a minister was a foregone conclusion. My call to the ministry was not blinding conversion, it was evolutionary personal development. God gave me the gifts for ministry, and I chose to be ordained in Christ's church.

I am a genealogical synthesis. My father is the Congregational Puritan, the churchman, the personality of the parish pastor—an intelligent, disciplined preacher. My mother is of southern stock, long on the oral tradition. She is a gifted but untutored writer and speaker. She senses the drama, the comedy, and the tragedy in the human situation. She is the storyteller and listener. She remembers the anecdotes and incidents of life and is moved by the arts, especially through storytelling. Growing up in her household, if I could interpret my childhood misbehavior with a good story my punishment was lessened. Maybe that is where I learned to tell good stories.

So, to be editor of *Ministry* was definitely providential. As is any editor, I was a gatekeeper: I controlled the flow of information. I could shape an emphasis or color an event or make something happen by the power of the word—my own words, or the words of others I had chosen to be published. And I was writing to, shaping, and directing my chosen profession: the ministry. The southern storyteller and the Pilgrim churchman in me were happy and satisfied, and to be content in one's work is a mellow experience. Providence was clearly working its inexorable force in my life. I had spent ten years in two parish churches, and at Christmas 1971 I was functioning as the editor in chief of a professional journal, "a first rate publication for a first rate profession," as we said in our pages. I lived that, I believed that, I was made mellow by that.

And, on that very night, up the stairs from the crackling fire shared with Margie and the satisfactions of important

work to do, were three cotton-topped heads—bedded
down with the supposed visions of sugarplums dancing.
Edward Michael was eight, a third grader, lover of sports
and school—a son to pass on the family name. Virginia
Ruth, named for her two grandmothers, was six, a first
grader, a child of gentle ways—ladylike even with messy
ice cream cones—and a possessor of good humor. She
made me laugh. And Mary Elizabeth, then three, named
for her paternal great-great-grandmother, the original
southern storyteller, and gifted with her mother's beauty
and smile—a happy child. They were the treasures of that
mellow night, the fruits of Margie's and my eighteen years
of life together. They were the reason for the warm, firelit
home, the promise of tomorrow, the rationale for doing
work with pride and living with character. On that night
the mellow mood was of the goodness of it all.

If I was emotional and mellow that Christmas Eve it was
because I am religious, and because I was thankful. We
had come home from our family church, the First Congregational Church of Western Springs, having sung the
carols of Christmas, heard the scriptures of the birth of a
savior, and meditated with our fellow members on the joy
of that first night and subsequent nights. I knew from
whence my blessings had come: They had come from the
Lord God who made heaven and earth. Life is in his
hands, and I was blessed by him.

My religion is a curious combination of ingredients. It is
scholarly and intellectual: The University of Chicago gave
me that. It is gentle, pastoral and articulate: My family
gave me that. It is pious and optimistic: Margie reinforces
that in me. It is mellow and joyful. I pray, but mostly I
pray prayers of thanksgiving, for I have good reason to be
thankful. I preach the gospel, but mostly the gospel I
preach is one of right doing, for right doing brings the

favor of God. I minister, but mostly I assure people that "this too shall pass away." I write, sometimes humorously, occasionally profoundly, because writing is one way God reaches me and, through me, I hope, others. God is my good friend, Jesus is my good teacher, and the world is my place of pleasant habitation.

The mellowness of Christmas 1970 was retrospective. Looking around my home and looking back over the years made me thankful, glad, and optimistic. In this moment I thought not of the future. Why should I? The future would be the continuity of the past. Providence was for me and not against me. This was the night of birth—let us rejoice and be glad in it.

But flickering flames cast not just light and warmth, they also produce shadows. Who knows what demons lurk in those darkened places?

Was that one flame or two I saw in the semi-darkness of that room?

Hey, Doc,
That Light Hurts!

The transformation of a thankful, robust young man into a bumbling, wounded elephant was neither easy nor swift. No magic wand passed over me nor was I changed in the twinkling of an eye. Instead of wands and twinkling eyes there were clinics and doctors and strange, exotic machinery and waiting, waiting, waiting.

Dr. Hackett, through my dilated pupil and his strong light, had seen into the back of my eye and what he saw there was bad. There was something that reduced the amount of light reaching the retina and thence the brain. It was blood.

The human eye is a marvelous creation—"the window of the soul," said Plato. But Plato had never been around opthalmologists. To them, and rightly so, the eye is an organ. It is nerve and muscle and cells. It is the object of their curiosity, the font of their knowledge, the beauty of their craft. But when all the rhapsodies are sung, the eye is an instrument, a means to an end. Humans see with their brains, not their eyes. The eye receives the stimulus of light, focuses on the sources of light, converts the light particles to nerve "signals" and, through the nerves of the retina, sends the signals to the brain for decoding, interpretation, and information to all the systems of the brain and body. It is marvelous how this works, and how little we are aware of the intricacies of this constant, continuous process—until the mechanism malfunctions.

There was blood inside my left eyeball. Where was it coming from? How did it get there? Would it stop? No one knew the blood was there except the doctor and me. It could not be seen from the outside. He knew it was there from the light he shone through my dilated pupil: objective verification. I knew it was there because everything grew dim when seen through that eye: subjective verification.

One night I lay in bed unable to sleep. In the dark of the room I tightly closed my right eye, struck a match, and held it above my head. I could see the light of the flame. Good, I was not blind. I decided to try an experiment. Closing my right eye tight and fixing my left eye in a stationary position, I moved the match from left to right with my hand above my prostrate head. I saw it on the left of my field of vision. Good. Then it came to the center, and my God, it disappeared! The bright light of the flame seemed to be extinguished before my very eyes. With my right eye still shut I kept on moving the match, and it emerged on the right side of my field of vision. What a shocking discovery. The flame came and went as it passed from left to right. I was so fascinated and horrified at this discovery that I burned my fingers. Unfortunately, the pain in my fingers convinced me this was not a dream. I did not wake up from the experiment. It was real. I could not see from the center of my left eye.

I told Dr. Hackett, whom I was seeing once a week, and he was not surprised. He expected it. I had a thousand questions for him. The big one was, "What's going on here?"

He did not usually talk much, but when I told him about the match experiment he sat back on his stool and crossed his arms. The time had come to talk. "Your vitreous humor has some plasmic occlusions in it," he began. Funny, he didn't look foreign, but he sure spoke another language. I asked him to translate. It seems that in the center of the eyeball there is a clear, jellylike substance (the vitreous humor). Light passes through the lens in the front of the eye, inverts the image (I remembered that from my high school general science class), and lands upside down on the back of the eyeball, where the rods and cones convert the light to nerve energy for the brain to decipher. That jelly in the eyeball is not part of the circulatory system—it does not flow in and out, it just sits there letting light beams stand on their head.

No doubt, you have heard the old toast, "Here's mud in your eye." That is sort of what I had: mud in my eye. No wonder everything looked dim in that eye: There was blood in the jelly. It couldn't go anywhere because of the absence of a circulatory system, and it just piled up there. But where was it coming from? How could we get it out so I could go back to seeing matches in bed at night? And other things.

Dr. Hackett went on about the physics of light and the wonders of the human eye, suddenly asking, "Did you ever live on a chicken farm?" What kind of a non sequitur was that! I told him no, and could we discuss agriculture another day? Right now I wanted to know how to get the blood out of my eye. Typically American—once we find a problem we fix it, right? If the eye is a mechanism, then oil the gears or replace the worn-out parts, right? Wrong. The eye is both tough and delicate. It does not yield to friendly persuasion or even crowbars.

Dr. Hackett wanted me to try something. He prescribed massive doses of cortisone. "Cortisone! You've got to be kidding, Doc! I won't take cortisone." "Why not?" he asked. I know what cortisone is, I bragged. In my work as a pastor I had called upon parishioners in the hospital who were taking cortisone. It stimulates the adrenal glands, and when you start messing with the glandular structure of the human body anything can happen. A little bit of science is a dangerous thing, and that little bit is what I have. A little bit of pastoral experience is a dangerous thing, too. I was a walking danger with all those little bits of knowledge.

He patiently explained that cortisone has the property of absorbing fluid in the body. "Did you ever hear of tennis elbow?" he analogized. Cortisone shots reduce the inflammation around the tendons—or is it the ligaments? (I told you I had just a little bit of medical information.) What a weird moment. I was sitting there with mud in the eye and he was telling me about tennis elbow and I was thinking cortisone would make me crazy. And what had any of that got to do with chicken farming?

On a subsequent visit a more sensible conversation unfolded. It seemed that some of the vessels in the back of my eye were "leaking." He couldn't see clearly where the leak was, and if he could clear out the cloudy particles in the ordinarily clear vitreous humor he could make a judgment about what to do next. The cloudiness, he said, might or might not go away eventually. It might perhaps pass through the eyeball by osmosis. But until it went out, not much more could be done. However, I didn't want to take cortisone if nature would get it out by itself.

So we waited, but there wasn't much change. It really wasn't too bad, I thought. Many people function very well with just one eye: Sammy Davis, Jr. had gone far with one eye. Maybe the Lord gives us a spare. I could still read and drive. The double vision persisted, but if I just closed the left eye it went away. Yankee ingenuity.

One small thing bothered me about the visits to Dr.

Hackett. He kept dilating and peeking into both eyes. Only the left eye couldn't see the match—why keep looking at the right as well? Was he addicted to those drops? I didn't ask him, and he didn't volunteer an explanation. I should have known: God made pairs, not spares.

You can make a career out of waiting in the lobby of opthalmologists' offices. They are always packed with people. Everyone seems to have eye problems. But Dr. Hackett made immediate appointments for me and wanted to insert me ahead of others still waiting. Such preferential treatment! Was it my winning personality? Was it the "Reverend" in front of my name? Or worse, was it the clinical interest he had in my eyeballs? Probably all three.

One day Dr. Hackett suggested that I see a colleague of his, a retinologist, he explained. I wondered if that was medical talk for chicken farmer. I had never heard of a retinologist, so I asked. Apparently retinology is a subspecialty of opthalmology, which is a subspecialty of optholaryngology, which is a subspecialty of general practice, which is a subspecialty of medicine. My gosh, you can't tell the players without a scorecard—or a Latin dictionary.

So, it was my retina and not my eye that was in trouble, but what did that mean? Subspecialists of subspecialists do not have offices in small towns, they have offices in large cities near large hospitals. Dr. Joel Kaplan was high up in an office building in downtown Chicago. I couldn't find his name on the building directory. Question: How come eye doctors use such small print? Must be good for business.

I waited in his office. Those folks were not there to get their eye lens prescription changed. In that office I was on the verge of a great discovery, only I didn't realize it and neither did the other anxious faces in the room. There are a lot of us in this world, a lot of us who are having serious visual difficulty. I am not alone, I am in a large group. But the group of us waiting in the lobby did not know we were a group. Each one of us was fighting his or her own battle, privately. We should have compared notes, not troubled glances.

Enter Brightlight Kaplan. He looked like a miner. He had strapped around his head one of those headlight things the anthracite miners wear. Was this a retinologist or a geologist? He, too, was on the dilation habit, only worse. His really made the world blur. Just when I could see practically nothing he leaned over me and turned on the miner's headlight. My God, it's a Hollywood premier and my retina is the star. But that light hurt. It was so strong I couldn't help tearing. We didn't chat much—it is hard to be convivial when you are undergoing the third degree for a crime you did not commit.

Dr. Kaplan wanted me to go to Michael Reese Hospital for some photography. This must be show biz and I am being given the big star buildup. "Photographs, what photographs?" I asked. "Of the back of your eyes," he explained. "I want to see those lesions." Now we were getting somewhere: Lesions were the problem. I started to go and he asked, "By the way, did you ever live on a chicken farm?" What was it with these doctors! I told him no, but I'm sure it's an honorable vocation.

Big-city hospitals are intimidating. Just reading the lists of departments sends a shiver down the spine when you recognize the incredible possibilities of what can go wrong with you. Photography was not listed on the directory, and I was almost surprised to discover it was in the department of opthalmology.

I was given a number. Big-city hospitals must be administered by mathematicians—they have a thing about numbers. I told a stone-faced nurse that I had an appointment,

and she told me to take a number and sit down. I had a
number, of course, because there was a long line of people
waiting for the photographer. Here we were again—an
even bigger crowd had assembled. The wait was long, and
this time I talked to the man next to me. He was a plumber
about my age. He couldn't discern the sizes of pipe he was
trying to link together. I learned he was there because his
doctor was worried about the other eye. The other eye?
You mean it's contagious! He knew as little as I did, and
together we formed a great pool of ignorance—and anxiety. But I liked him. He was the first "other" I had spoken
to who was like me. We probably could have organized a
homogeneous fellowship right there in that long waiting
corridor, but none of us was ready for interpersonal relationships. The magnitude of the hospital and our numbers
made us even more private. Who knew my name in there?
Who cared?

My anger was beginning to grow. It was joined by
panic. Why doesn't someone do something? Is it possible
that nothing can be done? Where is this thing going?
Maybe I should take the cortisone. I'm going crazy either
way.

The photography interested me. Since working on the
magazine I had gone in for some photography, with a Pentax Spotomatic camera. Any klutz can take pictures with
this model, the salesman had told me. I had resented the
implication, but his sales pitch was convincing. You can
imagine my surprise when I was finally ushered into a
room by the stone-faced nurse and there stood a man in a
white coat holding a Pentax Spotomatic camera. Any
klutz. . . . His camera had no lens on it, and he was filling
it with film. The lens, it turned out, was mounted on a
table. One was to sit behind the table and place one's fore-
head against a rubber-covered arc of steel and peer into

two tubes. I had played this game with both Hackett and Kaplan, but neither had said much over at the other end of the tubes. The camera was attached to one tube at a time. Boom, a great light would go off and the shutter would snap. The first time it was fun. By the fiftieth time it was damn annoying. The tubes, of course, were magnifying lenses and he was taking pictures of a very small portion of my anatomy. These pictures would be enlarged and the whole vascular structure of the eye could be seen by the doctor. Really terrific, if the vascular structure of the head of a pin is your thing. I preferred to stick to sunsets myself.

We finished the sitting and he called for "Stoneface." In she came with a long needle, and he asked me to remove my shirt. I started to explain that I gave blood to the Red Cross just the previous month, but I was no match for them. She jabbed the needle into my vein and boom, boom, the lights went off sequentially. Later I learned they had injected a phosphorescent dye into my bloodstream and were taking colored slides of the dye emitted from the leaking vessels in the back of my eyeball. It is a spectacular diagnostic tool. The phosphorescent dye passes through your whole body, including your kidneys. When the dye is in your body, your urine changes color. You may think your innards are corroding.

Back to Biglight Kaplan. There were different people in his waiting room that day, but they had the same anxious faces. Mine was anxious too. Four months had passed since the double-vision day in Washington, D.C., and nothing had been done for me except dilating my pupils, shining great lights in my eyes, and taking photographs. The match still disappeared, maybe even longer on its path from left to right.

Biglight did his thing again. I cried from the power of that light as he looked and looked into my pupils. But that day when he finished he wanted to talk with me. He had a large brown envelope in his hand, which contained eight-by-ten black-and-white glossies. The photos were the enlargements of the back of my eyeball. He wanted me to see for myself what was there.

Looking at the back of one's own eyeball is a strange experience. If I look at my hand I know it is my hand, because I can see and sense the connection to my torso. But the back of one's eye! That really is what Archie Bunker calls "the private parts." That may be the moment when I became an "expert" on the human eye. Previously I had seen or not seen, as the case may have been. But at that moment I had some clinical evidence of how that marvelous instrument, the human eye, is constructed, functions, or as I was about to see, malfunctions.

The photograph roughly resembled a map of Mars. There were many, many streams, rivulets, rivers, and canals following jigsaw patterns all over the photo. "This is a photo of the vascular structure of your eye," he said. So accustomed was he to the use of those pictures that he could not comprehend what a mind-boggling thing he had just shown and told me. He directed my attention to a dark, volcanolike area just slightly off center in the photo. "That is the macula," he said. I asked what that was, and because all his patients ask him that he had a ready answer. "The macula is the wallpaper on the front of the wall of the retina. Having wallpapered our kitchen not six months before, I could readily understand the metaphor. "All the light-sensitive tissue in the back of the eye reduces down into a cone, which becomes the retinal nerve transmitting the light signals to the brain. The macula is a thin membrane inside the eyeball located between the vitreous humor and the retina." Just call it wallpaper—it is easier to understand.

He showed me another photo, not my own. The black volcanolike hole was not there, or at least it was not as black or as deep as mine. The clinical evidence was beginning to mount: My macula, which until that very moment I did not even know I had, was in trouble.

I wanted to know what that trouble was. He pointed to some smaller black spots around the macula's center. "Those are the lesions," he said. "The blood vessels around the macula are hemorrhaging. That is where the blood in your eye has been coming from. The blood supply, which includes the nourishment and cleansing process necessary to support the cells in that thin membrane, has been cut off." The cells in the macula were dying, starving from the deprivation of their blood supply. That is why the match disappeared. It passed through a cemetery of dead tissue when I moved the flame from left to right.

A thousand questions popped into my mind, but the biggest one was, "What are you going to do about it?" "Mr. Kemper," he began, "if I were you I would take the cortisone. We need to stop that hemorrhaging." "All right. I will take the cortisone." The evidence of the need to do so was mounting and my options were diminishing. I had better take the chance. He prescribed a dosage that minimizes the side effects. I was to take twenty-four tablets every other day.

The first of many unpleasant dilemmas was upon me. There might be some adverse side effects from the cortisone, but if I didn't take it the hemorrhaging might continue, and where it would end God only knew. Margie told me about Kent Taylor, from the church. He had taken cortisone for an eye disease and it hadn't hurt him. So I called Kent, and it was true. He had not had any side effects and he saw well. I had the prescription filled.

Taking potentially dangerous medicine is very scary.

One holds the tablets in hand and administers a chemical that can change one's body, one's personality, one's life. I popped the pills in, probably because I suspected that my body, personality, and life were going to change whether I did it or not. And this had the possibility of helping.

I took the whole dose, and nothing adverse happened. Most of the things we worry about never come to pass.

Chasing the Dwindling Light through the Clinics

The anxious faces greeted me in Biglight Kaplan's waiting room in their accustomed manner: They ignored me. Poor Biglight, he really has a crummy job. I wouldn't like to look at anxious faces all day. In a way that was what I was beginning to do. When I looked into the mirror, I saw an anxious face. Surely I imagined it, but maybe once I saw a trunk growing between my two eyes.

I had not seen Biglight for about a month. I had noticed no changes since the cortisone, but I sure hoped he did. That day he really put the light into my eyes. It hurt, but maybe this time the miner would find some gold in there. That would be good news. I was hopeful.

He turned out the light, leaned back on the stool, and folded his arms to talk with me. That is what Dr. Hackett had done. They must teach body language in opthalmo-logical school. "The lesions are still there," he reported without emotion. I had paid the price: I had taken the cortisone. For the first time the unfairness of it hit me. Since I was a little boy I had been taught that if you do your duty you will be rewarded. What was the reward? The lesions were still there. I had expected a good sign, and he told me "no change." It wasn't fair.

"When is it going to start getting better, Doc? It has

been five months, and thousands of dilations and hours under your big light." (The more desperate I became, the more I exaggerated the facts.) "I think we had better do laser surgery soon," he replied. Laser surgery, now what the hell is that?! He didn't tell me what it was, but he explained what had to be done. "We (doctors, I have noticed, use *we* when they are not too sure of themselves) need to stop that hemorrhaging. Your eyesight will worsen if we do not." There it was again: the narrowing of the options. Damned if you do, damned if you don't. What kind of choice is that anyway?

"We have a new argonne laser beam at the University of Illinois Medical Center, where I teach, which may be effective in your case." There were too many troublesome words in that sentence: *New* means untried; *teach* means experiment; *may* means maybe yes and maybe no. I wanted it fixed!

"Look, Dr. Kaplan, if I have this laser surgery will I see normally again?" "No," he answered.

NO. What did he mean, "No"? If I let them mess around with my eyes I wanted some percentage of possible betterment.

"No, Mr. Kemper," he repeated, "the macular tissue is dead. We cannot bring that tissue back to life. It has been deprived of oxygen through the blood. The cells in the macula are destroyed. The laser cannot replace them."

God, I am a hopeless case. Dead tissue is dead tissue.

"Then, why do laser surgery if it will not restore dead tissue?" I asked him. He replied, "To keep the hemorrhaging from spreading further." He got out the photographs and showed me areas where the laser could "hit." "The beam of light will burn those leaking vessels and stop that process." "Burn the tissues," I said, "but you will kill those cells too." "Yes, but we will control the area of destruction. If we do not do that it may keep on growing. We cannot say for sure."

The clinical facts were beginning to dawn on me. I had been bleeding in the back of my eye. Nature stops the bleeding but the consequence is scar tissue. Scar tissue is opaque to light. That is why I could not see in the center of my left eye. The wallpaper had cast-iron sheets in front of it. As long as the hemorrhaging went on, the scar tissue would keep forming in a larger area.

I understood it, but I did not like what I understood.

The word *laser* terrified me. It is an acronym for Light Amplifications by Stimulated Emissions Radiated. That did not tell me much. It did not do much for me. It did not even raise the danger level of my little bit of knowledge. All I really knew about laser beams was that I once saw one used in a James Bond movie. In old-time movies the hero was in jeopardy when he was chained to a log heading for a buzz saw. In the James Bond movie he was tied to four inches of plate steel moving toward a laser beam. The beam cut the steel as if it were tissue paper. What would it to do Bond? What would it do to Kemper?

I called Dr. Hackett. "Kaplan wants to do laser surgery," I said. "Should I let him do it?" He said, in effect, "What have you got to lose?" I said, in effect, "A hole in my head."

"Dr. Hackett, I don't know Dr. Kaplan. He is not my friend. He hasn't hurt me, but on the other hand he hasn't helped me. I'm not sure I want a nonfriend of unknown efficiency burning out my eyeballs." Or something like that. "Why don't you get a second opinion?" Hackett asked. "Yeah, why don't I? What have I got to lose?" (Why did I keep saying that?)

Dr. Alexander Krill was the head of the department of opthalmology at the University of Chicago. Only the names and places had changed. I went through the same procedure. Long halls of anxious faces. More numbers and waiting. Same photography. Same miner's hat. Same bright light. Dr. Krill was the nation's foremost authority on histoplasmosis. The bad news was that I certainly should have the laser beam surgery.

I had not realized how important the business of giving a disease a name is to the practice of medicine. Diseases are known by awful Latin words, but the naming is very important. Once you name a disease you can predict its course and treatment. If you cannot name it accurately you may be surprised or wrong. I should have known this about the power of names. Baptism is a significant rite in Christendom. In the Bible, people's names mean something: "You shall call his name Immanuel, meaning God with us." Names are important in medicine and religion.

But this disease of the macula had not yet been baptized. According to the expert, it was not histoplasmosis. My parents would be glad to know that—they thought it their fault that I was born in the Mississippi Valley. "Let us just say it is a form of macular degeneration," Dr. Krill had concluded. "We do not know what it will do, but the laser should reduce its spread. The important thing is to save the other eye."

Save the other eye! No one had said that before. The other eye was fine—it passed the match test every night. The other eye? How would the world look through *two* eyes with holes in the middle? Perish the thought. That would make me worse off than Sammy Davis, Jr.

"All right, Dr. Kaplan, make an appointment for laser surgery." He would do it when he returned from vacation. What a time to take a vacation. Doctors must be the most traveled professionals in the world—they are always off somewhere. It must be necessary relief from those anxious faces all the time.

Dr. Kaplan did have a suggestion for the interim.

Would I be willing to go to the University of Illinois Eye and Ear Infirmary next week? I could meet Dr. Goldberg, the head of the department, and if I would be so kind I could be there for "rounds." He didn't say so, but there were a couple of implications in the invitation. One was that my disease was enough of a novelty to attract the attention of medical students. The other was that if I would be part of the clinical process, the considerable fees involved might be handled in another, more favorable, way. In short, guinea pigs are cheap. So why not do it? What have I got to lose? (Gee, I wish everyone would stop saying that.)

I could tell I was at the university clinic for eye research: the same anxious faces. I felt I was becoming a groupie—my crowd was everywhere. Same dilation. But there was a new wrinkle this time around. I was placed in a curtained, dark cubicle. In the cubicle next door was an Irish setter. Jumping Jehosophat, what was a nice guy like me doing in a place like that? It seemed the Irish setter was blind, a victim of a rare genetic fluke. Very interesting to fledgling opthalmologists. Speaking of fledgling opthalmologists, there they were. Five hundred miners' lamps peered into my eyes. (I told you I exaggerate when I am anxious.)

I should have known what to expect. I should have because I teach preaching to seminary students. One does not begin the craft of preaching as a polished orator, one begins fumblingly and faultily. That has to be true of every craft, discipline, and profession. But in my naïveté I never expected that of doctors. What klutzes these beginners were. One couldn't get his front light to shine. One looked at the wrong eye and said "Aha!" One asked me if I ever lived on a chicken farm—jeez, they start them young. The last to look spent a long time peeking into my eyes. Then he sat back and said, "Very interesting, Mr. Kemper.

Now, where is the dog?" The Irish setter and I went home confident that we had contributed to the advancement of medical science, and boy, did those beginners need advancement! "Keep them out of the operating room," I told Dr. Goldberg. "Don't worry," he said.

I worried anyway.

The day for the laser surgery had arrived. I hoped Kaplan had found smiling faces in Acapulco. I didn't know what to expect. He had said I needn't be hospitalized—that was good. But also that I shouldn't make plans for the evening—that was bad.

My groupies were there. I had come to welcome those anxious faces. I was shown into a small room with a couple of chairs and a kind of kitchen table, on which sat a large, impersonal machine. With dilated pupils I sat there watching that black monster fade and distort like some special effect from a science fiction movie. "Please God, let this not be science fiction."

Kaplan and Krill came in. No white coats, no surgical masks—this was not going to be like Marcus Welby. I took a chair at the table, with the two surgeons on the other side. A large, slightly uncomfortable contact lens was put on my left eye. I put my head into the chute, as I had done so many times before. Now, hold your head still, I was told. With what I knew from James Bond, I wouldn't have moved my head had the building tumbled down around me. In the ruins they would have found a terrified young man staring into a big, black impersonal machine.

Whack! A great burst of blue-green light went off in my head: a personal lightning storm, without the thunder, in front of my very own eyes—or inside my very own eyes. I felt nothing, heard nothing, smelled nothing—not even smoke from the burning tissue in the back of my eyeball.

Ninety-two times the lightning struck. There was never a flicker or hint of pain. That big black monster was merciful—or Kaplan and Goldberg knew how to make it so.

It was done. A patch was placed on my left eye, and I was sent home. I felt fine. I saw well out of my right eye and was released from Dr. Kaplan's care unless I should notice any change.

Deck Chairs on the Titanic

Six months is not a long time in one's normal life-span. It is longer than a semester in school, but shorter than a pregnancy. But those first six months of 1972 were days of stress for me and my family.

Stress of this sort is not constant, unremitting. The problem with my eye was up front in my consciousness, but it was not all that was there. Other things, events, people passed through my consciousness. In those days I did not yet think of myself as an elephant; I was not yet aware of the strange metamorphosis under way. Rather, I thought of myself as wounded. I had been hurt, but not slain; I had been affected, but not changed. Everybody has experiences with wounds. They hurt, they are potentially dangerous, they need attention and time for healing. I was doing what sensible people do: I had seen competent medical personnel, had received their treatment and advice. I had met the situation as well as one meets any untoward situation.

Meantime, life went on in a reasonably normal fashion. The summer interlude, six months after the day in the Senate gallery, six months after the mellow Christmas mood, brought me time for reverie and stocktaking. Despite the eye problem, I had been reasonably productive.

In February I had scored what for me was the greatest coup of my fledgling journalistic career. I had gone to Claremont, California, where I interviewed Peter

Drucker, the famed author and lecturer. *The Christian Ministry* was taking a fresh look at the six functional areas of the parish ministry: preaching, teaching, planning, counseling, managing, and public action. In each issue we presented an in-depth interview with a distinguished person in one of those functional areas. I had wanted to interview Peter Drucker for the management issue, but he was known to give very few interviews. He has a theory that once one becomes a public figure and is interviewed and goes on talk shows, one becomes a celebrity and must satisfy a public—which is a detraction from the work one wants to accomplish.

About a year earlier I had reviewed his latest book, *The Age of Discontinuities*, for *Ministry*. I had sent him a copy of the review with a note about the importance of his thought for practicing church leaders, and his gracious thank-you note included a fateful phrase. He said he had been disappointed that no one had seen the religious implications of his work. His own Episcopal Church had never used him, and most of his time was spent consulting with not-for-profit, voluntary organizations. That was all I needed to know to seek his agreement for an interview. I would give him plenty of space to talk to religious leaders about more effective methods of leading not-for-profit, voluntary organizations.

We spent a day together at his home in Claremont, California. Despite the affected one eye I could still fly to Los Angeles, rent a car, wend my way through the maze of freeways, tape-record a conversation (having read many of his books in advance so I would know what to ask him), and then spend days editing the transcript into a useful and succinct interview/article.

I did that work with great enthusiasm and joy, and am still proud of the result. Further, I did it with only one eye functioning normally. Could the reading, writing, driving be done with both eyes gone? Never, but that was the relative happiness of that point in time. I may not have been normal, but I was highly functional.

In those summer reveries I realized with some satisfaction that I was beginning to build a reputation and a following. I had some promising invitations for the future: to preach in the chapel of Wittenburg University, and to address the thousands of clergy at the Ohio Pastors' Convention. I had several article assignments, and a book was being discussed. I had been elected to the board of trustees for my alma mater, Chicago Theological Seminary, because of special expertise in religious communications. I was also to give the commencement address the following spring, later canceled due to the uproar caused by the Cambodian incursion.

Those special invitations and honors were very important to me. They may not have seemed much to another, but I was only thirty-seven and was being asked to do things that I had admired in others for most of my life. I was writing, teaching, lecturing to my fellow clergy. For more than ten years I had consumed that fare, and now I was being a producer. It was a heady experience, and I thrived on it. So what if I had one bad eye. It didn't stop Sammy Davis, Jr., why should it stop me?

Margie, the children, and I were happy with our life in Western Springs. It was good to be home in that suburban village southwest of Chicago. Neither of us was native to the village, but about ten years earlier we had lived there for a year. While a student at the Federated Theological Faculties, I was required to suspend formal academic study and spend an entire year in a parish, and had been assigned to the First Congregational Church of Western Springs. It was a chancy development. At first, it did not

seem to be an exotic assignment. My classmates were in
Greenwich Village and San Francisco and there I was,
twenty miles away from the campus in a staid suburb.
But, in retrospect, it was providential that I was assigned
to that particular congregation.

The intern year had been sensational. The senior minister of the church (the position I now hold) was Dr. Edward
F. Manthei, the one parish minister aside from my father I
most admired. He was a great preacher, highly literate,
and a caring person. I carry in me to this day much that
was first demonstrated in the person of Ed Manthei. (So
important was he to me that my son is his namesake.) As
an intern I was a student-in-residence. I was expected to
perform the full range of ministerial services, albeit fledgling and green. But it was the people of First Congregational Church who gave me support and encouragement.
The Women's Society furnished our apartment—it was the
first home Margie and I ever had, having been married but
a few months when first we arrived. I was the superinten-
dent of the sixth grade Sunday school class, and as such
was the resource person for some really fine lay teachers:
Bob Vogele, Milt Eastman, John Hilton, Harriet Euson—
all of whom are now parishioners of mine. I attended all
the board and committee meetings and I preached in the
pulpit—all things I do now day in and day out. It was like
a preview of my future fifteen years before it happened.

During the summer of 1972 I was in my second incarna-
tion at that church, and it was good too. I was a quasi-lay
member of the congregation, in that I was an ordained
minister of the United Church of Christ (the proper
denominational name of former Congregational churches)
doing special religious work as editor of *Ministry*. I was
not a parish minister, in other words, but I was a minister.
When I accepted the editorial position I had an experience

unique for a parish minister: Editorial assignments, unlike parish churches, did not come with parsonages. After serving two churches, one in Newton Falls, Ohio, and one in Montclair, New Jersey, for the first time I had to provide my own housing and could live wherever I wanted. And when Margie and I thought of moving to Chicago and choosing a place to live, there was only one place we wanted to be: Western Springs, as First Congregational Church would be our home church. When it was known in Western Springs that we wanted to move back to town, Ken Seim, the senior minister at the time, and Neatsy Groton sent us local papers so we could see the real estate ads, and we bought a home through an agent, Myron Ash, we had known well fifteen years before. Our children were enrolled in the church's nursery school to be taught by teachers we had known before. On the Sunday we joined the church we were greeted and welcomed by so many familiar faces—the Klinderas, the Mensens, the Prices— from our days with the M & M Club in the church of fifteen years before. To us, these were not just church members, they were old friends. Indeed, in the summer days of 1972 had I to name my closest and best friends, they would be found in the church directory.

Thus, this "one-eyed Jack" found himself doing work he was proud to do, living in a town of his choosing, surrounded by church friends, and engaged in relationships that had a history and a meaning. I might have been wounded, but with so much going for me surely I would recover. I was not yet an elephant, just a one-eyed fellow who still could enjoy life and relationship and work.

That summer I drove Margie and the three children to Tower Hill Camp in southwestern Michigan. It was to be the last summer I would drive them there or anywhere. My parents joined us from southern Illinois for a couple of days, sensing they should spend some time with me that summer. They did not know why they should and I didn't either, but they came and it was good to be with them. My mother had always practiced medicine without a license, and she was in a horrible dilemma. Her maternal love made it almost unbearable for her to inquire about my eyes, but her medical curiosity wanted all the clinical details. After hearing them she was interested, but not relieved. I discovered around the edges of the conversation that she was very worried. When she is worried she does sneaky things, like calling up opthalmologists to find out what my symptoms meant. I would not have wanted to be her opthalmologist—she probably drove him crazy with questions he could not answer. I knew what she was going to say, but I let her say it anyway: She recited my whole history of medical maladies. "Do you remember how we were careful to close the drapes when you had the measles?" she asked. "Yes, Mother, I remember." And I did, but it was irrelevant. Her medical inventory came to the same conclusions as mine, and Hackett's and Kaplan's and every other physician I had seen, viz., there was nothing extraordinary in my case history. I was healthy as an eleph . . . as a horse. Her second field of research took her into the family history, and she had spoken at length with the eldest member of the family. The best she could discover was that a few of my ancestors wore glasses. In other words, my case was unprecedented. So my mother had two prescriptions. First, I was to take vitamins. And just in case I wouldn't take this to heart she had purchased a case and hauled them to Michigan for me to begin at once.

Her second prescription was prayer. She wanted me to know of prayer chains then under way for me. She had written to prophets and evangelists of all sorts and types to have them pray for me. And she and my father were in constant prayer. I was gratified by the report. She knew this was something she could do for me and she left no prayer unturned in seeing it was done.

My own prayers were not either desperate or effective to this point. I am a bit unusual about prayer in these matters—somehow I never want to trouble God with trivial matters. I am long on gratitude but short on requests for myself. My prayers have been of the "If it be Thy will, let this cup pass from me" nature. I had not allowed my eyes to be a test case for God's compassion. I already believed in that, and it did not have to be proven again.

So, the summer went by with happy hours on the beach with the children, games in the cottage, good food, and happy talk. I wished my eye disease had not happened, but it had and I would make the best of it. My thoughts were mostly on the goodness of the moment and the prospects of the future. After all, I was a functioning human being, not a bumbling elephant.

The Double Image Becomes a Mirror Image

When summer was over I was ready for a heavy fall schedule. I had been advised I could not hurt my eyes by use, so I expected to do all my usual reading, writing, preaching, traveling.

The first stop on my fall tour was Merom, Indiana, where a group of clergy on retreat had wanted me to make an evening address. I did this a lot since becoming editor of a professional journal. When I was a parish minister myself, I wasn't an expert. The title must have made the difference. Merom is way south of Indianapolis, virtually inaccessible by plane. I told Margie I wanted the car, and drove the long, long way down toward the Wabash River, about two hundred miles from home. It was a sunny fall early afternoon. The country was pretty. I thought about my speech, which was written out in my customary manuscript form; I would place it on the lectern and read my well-turned prose. I would probably do well, and expected to be late getting back home. "Let's see, if I finish by 8:00 P.M., I'll be back by midnight. Maybe I can sleep a little later tomorrow."

I gave the speech. I was right—my prose was well written and well delivered. I dashed out the door to the polite applause that clergy grudgingly give other public speakers, and climbed into the car for the four-hour ride home.

"Jimminy, it is dark out here in the boondocks. This road really winds and turns through these hills. Hey, I missed my turn back there. I didn't see the road sign."

I did not see the road sign. How could I miss that? It was as plain as the nose—or was it the trunk—on my face. I was not seeing well that night. The ride was horrible. I was only going thirty miles an hour; I would never get home. Panic hit me: Something was changing. I was at Gary by midnight and home by three. I did not have a St. Christopher statue in my car, but I think the saints brought me home safely.

The next day was not bright and sunny like the day before, it was cloudy and gray. I saw better than I had at night but not as well as I had by day. I bought my usual paper for the commute on the train. I could read the headlines and had to hold it close to read the small type.

God help me, the same symptoms and syndrome with the other eye.

It was the same all over again, a kind of mirror image of the previous six months. It was Kaplan and Goldberg. Dilation and lights that hurt. Photography. And waiting, waiting, waiting. The groupies were still there, still anxious. I was one with them. Like Pinocchio, my trunk grew longer—only I could not see my image in the mirror. It was just as well that I could not see my self-image, because I would not have liked it. I had fallen behind Sammy Davis, Jr.

I could not read at all, under any circumstances. The train ride, which I had loved because I could read the first two of my four daily papers, was a long drag of sitting and staring out the window. My work was a mess. My assistant, Joan Lichterman, held it together. She read manuscripts, edited, made my decisions, but lovely person that she is, she talked to me about everything so I could feel I was doing the work. I tried to talk to my boss and friend, Alan Geyer, at the Christian Century Foundation. He did not want to talk about my future: "Wait and see what happens," he advised. Meantime, I knew he worried about me, and about what to do about me. It is tough to be a boss and a Christian.

My friend, Bob Karsten, called and wanted to know my travel plans for coming to Springfield, Ohio. He was chaplain of Wittenburg University and expected me to preach in the chapel on Reformation Sunday—a big blast day for Lutherans, and I was to be chief trumpeter. I told him I thought I could not come. He insisted; I promised. Joan said, "Go—what have you got to lose? Dictate your sermon to me and I will type it in capitals. You'll do fine." "I guess I'll try it. Shoot, anyone can preach one good sermon."

Getting to Springfield was no big deal. I would fly to Dayton, and Bob would meet me there on Saturday. I saw well enough to be mobile. It was only the center of the eye—both eyes—that had been darkened. I still had some peripheral vision, and because I kept moving my head and eyes around I could see most of my environment. I had my trusty tape recorder with me, Joan's large-type manuscript, and a heart full of trepidation.

Bob met me and placed me in the dormitory for a good night's sleep before Sunday's chapel. I found a small magnifying glass in a drawer in my room. Had Bob and Joan been talking behind my back? Anyway, I used it. I took her large type, read it with the magnifying glass, and tape-recorded my reading. I could hear it back again. Fortunately, I have a good ear—crummy eyes, but a good ear. I fell asleep listening to that sermon for the one hundred and fifty-first time. I was anxious again.

It was a beautiful day, a beautiful chapel, a beautiful

large congregation. It was time to preach. I climbed a long staircase to the immense elevated pulpit. "This will go over their heads," I amused myself thinking, as I climbed onward and upward to my isolation booth. I put the manuscript down on the lectern and stood tall to preach.

"God, I am too far away from the manuscript!" I had practiced sitting down with the manuscript, magnifying glass and eyes about eighteen inches apart. I was twice as far away from the manuscript. I dared not pick it up and whip out the magnifying glass. I began. The words from the tape recorder were playing in my ears and coming out of my mouth. Yes, I remembered the introduction. I remembered the first point and illustration. "Now, what was the second one? Dear God, what was the second point?" I could not remember it. I was panicky. I shifted the pages of the manuscript, but they were blank to my eyes. I could not read them. I could not read them! I could not preach. The silence was awful. They all looked at me. I perspired, I felt faint. The silence was unbearable.

I stammered a few words from scripture, commented briefly on them, and said the benediction. To them it was an incredibly short sermon. To me it was the longest sermon of my life, because I felt it to be the last sermon of my life. I would never embarrass God, friends, and self that way again. The pulpit was no place for an elephant.

Bob was kind, but we both knew he was lying. He sensed my pain but could do little for it but be there. I was glad for that. But there it was. Lou Gehrig's last day as a Yankee. Clark Gable's last movie. Mayor Curley's last hurrah. It was over. I would never preach again.

God damn it all.

Back in Chicago, I told Alan I would resign as editor as soon as I could find out what I needed to do to draw Social Security. I asked Margie's father what savings and loans do when you default on mortgage payments. I snarled at Margie because she had let her teacher's certificate lapse. I talked to God only when I wanted him to curse something: me, it, them, everything. Elephants do not belong in editorial offices, financial offices, homes, or churches. They are too damn clumsy, good for nothing.

I was really on the ropes. No one could believe what had happened. Alan, Joan, Margie, my parents, her parents: All believed there was help somewhere. "There has to be someone, somewhere in this country who knows what to do for you." I finally agreed to ask Dr. Hackett if he knew some other doctor. He said I had had the best care at the Chicago universities, and that was as good as there is anywhere. I pleaded with him; there must be other places. I would go anywhere, do anything. I am not exaggerating this time when I say I was anxious. God, was I anxious.

Hackett said, "There is Dr. Donald Gass at the Bascom Palmer Eye Institute in Miami, Florida. He has treated thousands of cases like yours, but he won't be able to do you any good." I didn't care. I'd go. Make me an appointment. What have I got to lose? Now *I* was saying it.

My ministerial friend, Dick Bailar, met me at the Miami Airport. "Where's your white cane, Kemper?" he said with a smile. That's my friend Bailar—as genuinely helpful as he is tactless. I like him, and he helped a lot on this last-ditch visit.

The groupies were in Florida. There we were in the halls of another large hospital. The procedure began again: the drops, the lights, the photography. Maybe I should go into the eye-examining business—in the previous year I must have become a pro. I could do better than the doctors. (Still anxious.)

Finally, I saw the Great Man, the Last Hope, the Savior. Fortunately for him, he did not know he was all those

things to me. He would have run away from me, but he
did not know or run. He looked at me straight on and
said, "Mr. Kemper, I have studied all your tests and
reports. You have a form of macular degeneration. There
is an 80 percent chance it will stay the way it is forever;
there is a 10 percent chance it will worsen; there is a 10
percent chance it will slightly improve. You will not go
totally blind. The damage to your central vision is permanent, irreparable, and irrevocable. There is nothing more
we can do for you."

"But Doc, what do I do now?"

"You learn to live with it."

THE ELEPHANT
TRIES TO DANCE

Bon Voyage

Dr. Gass had sure turned out to be a bust. Or had he?

What had he done? How had he affected me? He had disavowed the role I had created for him. He had not known that of course, but that is what he did. I went there for salvation, and he had said, "I cannot heal you." The role he had played was the role he felt comfortable in: that of clinician. He looked at the evidence before him, and he rendered a judgment. That is what he was qualified to do—what, in fact, I had asked him to do. He simply did it. He had said: "The evidence is that you have macular degeneration. It seems to have run its course. There is nothing more to be done for it, and therefore, nothing more to be done for you."

He did not offer me help, hope, or healing. I guess that is not the clinician's field. I have heard doctors make impassioned speeches about not being God. I always believe them when they say it. I believe them because of the context in which they say it—one of desperation, when their science is up against the limits, when their craft knows no more alternatives. Then, they disavow divinity. But they are not consistent. In other contexts they play god-parts all the time—and love the role. In primitive society when the authority of the witch doctor was threatened, he introduced more mumbo jumbo. When one is the keeper of The Secrets and someone challenges the way one keeps the secrets, a good smoke screen will make the person think twice about the challenge. Doctors do that today. So do clergy. It is unprincipled on the part of both professions, but they do it.

Looking back on it, I have to appreciate the way the doctors—all of them—steadfastly refused to promise me anything, not even hope for a better tomorrow. They were always very matter-of-fact. Clergy are not that way. They promise you things for which you do not even ask. It is hard not to be assuring. If you have an ounce of compassion you want to allay fears, wave hands, kiss frogs that turn out to be restored human beings. Who does not want to do that? The problem with most doctors is not lack of will. They want to see you restored—it is good for their business.

No, the problem is the clinical method. When they see something over and over, know over and over what course it will take and that they are powerless to make it otherwise, many doctors say nothing. They are in conflict between their compassion and their clinical projections. The best doctors are those who know they suffer those tensions, but then ask: What is the best course for this patient? That is what Dr. Gass did for me. He decided to do what was best for this patient. And what was best was to tell me straight on that my string had run out, I had reached the end of the line. There was no Messiah to deliver me.

The problem doctors have is not just the tension between compassion and predictable evidence. The tougher problem is the patient's projections onto the doctor. It is the patient who surrenders his power to the doctor. Sure, some doctors are intimidating. But many are not, and still the patient surrenders his personal power. "Heal me, O mighty one" should be a biblical prayer, but more often than not it is the contract between patient and doctor. In some instances, healing will not happen until the patient regains some of the power he had lost in the process of transformation, power he had given to doctors in the hope for recovery.

That was my problem. And that is what Dr. Gass told me: *You* learn to live with it. That was his compassion for me. I needed to be freed from the physicians' power. Good advice, and potentially creative. But there was one snag. Even freed, learning to live with it was my problem in an even more powerful way. In leaving behind science and the clinics, my problem became the struggle for rehabilitation. The elephant needed to dance and to learn the ballet. And would the doctor see the elephant through the next steps? No, he would not. It was my problem, not his problem.

Maybe doctors do this because of the next anxious face that will enter their room: Perhaps his case is different— the evidence isn't so sure. Maybe they will heal this wounded veteran. I like to think it is the doctor's discipline to stick to the clinical evidence in the hope of finding the cure that makes the quandary disappear. But I harbor another, more sinister, suspicion. It may be that doctors will not accept rehabilitation as their problem because to accept that is to accept scientific failure. If science is true and right, then why could not this patient's eyes have been healed before the damage was done? That is the cue for the "not being God" speech.

But I am speaking of something more profound. I am speaking of the doctors' inability to accept failure. We, with unhealed eyes, are an embarrassment to those who heal eyes. That is the sinister motive I harbor about doctors: They are afraid to fail. That should trouble gods, not mortals.

The evidence I submit for harboring this sinister view is

that not one of my doctors knew what I would need for rehabilitation. "That is beyond the purview of my competency," they said. "Nonsense," said I. "Good patient care goes beyond the clinic, beyond telling the patient the truth about his condition. It goes on to walk those first few, faltering steps with the wounded. The wounded will have to walk alone, of course, or surely they will never dance again. But come on, doctors, go a few steps. At least know what helps are around for rehabilitation."

That last day in the Bascom Palmer Eye Institute with Dr. Donald Gass was another of those momentous days. It was like the day almost a year before in the Senate gallery, only this day I was not seeing double. I was seeing nothing at all in the center of both eyes. Like that year, however, I was unaware and hence ill-prepared for what would happen next, how I would meet it, and what would become of me. I must be a slow learner. I never seem to spot the beginnings when I am at the beginning. It is always hindsight, not foresight, that tells me what is or is not a momentous day.

This was a day of leave-taking. This day I would say goodbye and I would say hello. I would say hello to people, things, and experiences. I would say goodbye to dilated pupils, bright lights that hurt, laser machines that did not hurt but looked like they could, stone-faced nurses, white-coated doctors and medical students, Irish setters, and the much-revered chicken farm. I would say hello to the thrashings of elephants, the psychic sweat of effort and the tears of failure, the fellowship of the church, and the outstretched arms of many who would wish me well and would help to make me well.

Although I did not know it or understand it, all this leave-taking was symbolized. I shook hands with Dr. Gass and said goodbye, and walked down the hall to meet Dick

Bailar. I shook hands and said hello to this friend and minister of the church. It was the changing of the guard. I was walking from science to religion. They may not be much further apart than those few steps down the corridor, but sometimes it takes an elephant a long time to find his way.

Bailar asked how it went and I lied, "About what I expected." He said, "You know, Kemper, I've been sitting here watching all these wretches bumping into things and holding on tight to others and looking lost. You look, act, and get around better than any of these bums." That's Richard: tactless, but helpful.

Taking Inventory and Making Resolutions

The flight back to Chicago was again time for inventory.

I knew then I was an elephant, but no one else on the plane did. Bailar got me to the right gate, and I managed the tickets, seat assignments, seat belt fastening, and everything else. There I was: an elephant strapped down and no one else knew it. The symbolism was staggering.

Beginning this inventory, what I saw was everything in general and nothing in particular. How could I explain that to people? Well, I could tell them that cookies look like doughnuts to me—I miss the center because of the blind spots in the center of my eyes. That was true, but would people understand that when they see me reach easily for a cookie on a tray, pick it up, and put it in my mouth? I could read nothing—oh, maybe a banner headline on a newspaper, or a big sign if I were up close to it. I could do those things through peripheral vision. If the print were big enough I could discern the letters with the vision around the center. I had to stop driving. I could see the curb to the right and the lane marking to the left, but there in the center I saw nothing. Is that a child darting out there? Is that a stalled semi-truck trailer in the lane ahead of me? I couldn't say, and if I couldn't say then I ought not be driving. I could see human beings around me. I could discern male and female (except for some of the unisex getups), tall or short, skinny or fat, very young or very old. But I could not tell the particulars that make each person unique. Are they smiling or frowning? Are they blonde or brunette? Are they talking to me or to someone else near me?

While doing this inventory I was discovering something strange and wonderful. This didn't just start on the flight home, it had been going on for a few months. But I was becoming conscious of it and that made it seem wonderful and new. I was adapting. Not I as a person, but my eyes were adapting. Those eyes wanted to see—everything, all of the time. The stewardess brought me dinner. I wanted to see her face, and by moving my eyes right and left I could see her features. I was not even conscious of the nerves and muscles around the eyeballs that pull the eyes ever so slightly one way or the other so that what was in the middle would appear to me. It was the reverse of the old match experiment. By holding the match stationary over my head and letting my eyes move from side to side, I could see it most of the time.

What a great discovery it was to know that those eyes, wounded as they were, had not given up. Those unthinking, unfeeling orbs had an intentionality that my thinking, feeling psyche did not: They wanted to make do with what they had. They would not quit trying to see. Had they thought or felt as I did they would probably have been angry and scared as I was, but they moved to the direction of other stimuli. Would that I were in touch with that same energy and power!

Noble as my unthinking, unfeeling eye tissues were, they were still playing strange tricks. Every so often a bright flash would go off in my eyes, a cometlike spiral that thinned and burned out as it twisted and turned. It was blue-green like the laser beam. The first few times I saw those things I thought, "Now what?" Of course I was skittish about everything I saw. They turned out to be retinal tensions. The laser had burned the tissue in the back of the eyes, and it tightened or puckered as it healed. That's what those lights were: tissue healing from the wounds. My eyes were getting along better than I was.

Despite the unthinking adaptability of my eyes, I learned they still had to get their visual information to the rest of my system. For instance, the airline dinner tray provided an unpleasant emotional experience. The little cups of cream and of dressing both looked alike to my wounded but struggling eyes, and I had poured the cream onto my salad and the salad dressing into my coffee.

The strapped-in elephant who put salad dressing in his coffee was coming home.

How Do You Tell
Bad News?

We should have kept the trip to Miami a secret. We had told everybody that I was going to see a doctor who might be able to help, and then everybody who knew about the potential wanted a report on the actual.

Margie got the first long report. I told her the whole story—there was not a thing that could be done, I was stuck with it—and it was hard to tell how she took the news. She had wanted me to go, and maybe she knew it would be to no avail. She was looking for a signal about how I felt about it, and I was looking for a signal about how she felt. With all that signal-watching not much communication took place. But, then, what was there to say? As Tevye had put it, "It's a fact."

After telling the results to Margie in some detail, I hadn't the heart to repeat them. But I had to. Her parents called. My parents called. Our friends called. The neighbors came over. Distant relatives called. My boss called. I was really tired of talking and wanted to be alone for a while. I wanted to think. Another discovery was dawning, not so momentous as those in Washington or Miami, but true nonetheless: Partially blind people have trouble being left alone. Either they have to have someone with them or someone wants to be with them. At least it seemed so to me in the early days.

The news from Miami was told on the phone and in person. The more I told it, the less I told. The final version was, "Oh, not much happened." In a way that was true, but in another way it just meant I had moved one step beyond the momentous moment.

I noticed something interesting about people. When I told them face to face there was nothing more to be done, they always said, "Boy, you sure look terrific." On the other hand, when I told people by phone they would say, "Surely there is someone else somewhere who can help you." I do not know what to make of that observation. Probably nothing—or is it true that seeing is believing? When people saw me telling the bad news, they believed it; when they only heard, they refused to accept it.

I had the most trouble telling my parents. Bless their hearts, they loved me so much they wanted all to be well. It is the curse of parenthood that one never relinquishes responsibility for one's children, even when they are responsible for themselves. My parents somehow felt it was their fault that my eyes were shot. The thought had never occurred to me. But they spent hours going over my childhood health and that of our ancestors, drudging up trivia from the past to find some clue to the present. I wished they hadn't because I knew nothing would come of it, but they did it because they loved me and wanted the best for me.

I hated to tell Alan Geyer at *The Christian Century*. He had gone out on a limb for me a couple of times. He had decided to start *The Christian Ministry* because I had said the ministerial profession needed it and wanted it, and it was he who had offered me the editorship, even though I didn't know a sans serif from a pica. That was a lot of trust in me. Thousands of dollars were spent on the new venture, and to make matters worse, things were not too good for the whole operation. Jimminy, look how I had complicated life for Alan Geyer and the Christian Century Foundation. I was beginning to feel guilty for something I could not control and had not created.

There was one special group to whom I hated to have to tell my bad news, and that was a small group of intimate friends. The night before I had left for Miami they had a surprise party for me—really a surprise; I had not suspected a thing. We had been invited to the Warners' for dinner, and when we were ushered into the living room about twenty couples jumped out and shouted, "Surprise!" It might sound like a dumb moment, but I had really needed them that night. Each had brought some silly little gift just to let me know I was being remembered. I imagine they will never know how much that thoughtfulness meant to me.

They probably thought it was a simple gesture to give that going-away party, and to them it was. But to me, it was much more. The real pain I was beginning to feel was not physical, it was spiritual. It was a loss of self-esteem. That thing I call the elephant was really a big creature, with a shriveled self-image. He did not think well of himself. He felt guilty. He felt inadequate. He felt unable to cope. Those are surefire self-esteem problems, and when in the midst of those growing hurts your friends rally to a testimonial party which says they care about you, can anything be more helpful at that moment?

With friends like that, who needed doctors?

Why Is Daddy So Grouchy?

The mellow mood of Christmas 1970 had hardened by midsummer of 1972. Eighteen months is not long in the life-span of a mature human being, but when that human being is becoming an elephant it can seem forever. Just a few months before I had been thankful to God for my work, my home, my wife, my children. Then came fingernail time. I was hanging onto a full, productive life by my fingernails—and even those were frayed from the stress of biting.

It is true that on the plane back from Miami I had resolved to try harder, and that I was doing. Fervently and doggedly, I expected to triumph over my loss of full vision by sheer effort. But one crack in the armor of attack was becoming painfully clear to me. The strategy was intensely personal: It was *my* problem, and only I had the resources to overcome it. That was true as far as it went. The problem was that "the I" went further than just myself.

It was John Donne who wrote that no man is an island—a simplistic platitude that I had used in countless sermons when I wanted profundity but had none of my own to give. Of course no man is an island. No elephant is an island either. Just because I had suffered a transforming wound did not mean that I had at that instant also ceased the functions of life. This elephant's island was surrounded by others. I was still a husband, still a father, still a home-owner, still a workman, still a minister of Christ's church. All that I had been, I still was.

But the enormous effort I was spending to rehabilitate myself was taking a toll—a price was being exacted from others important in my island's life.

The ugly truth of the moment was that I was carrying a heavy load of anger beneath my thick elephant's hide. Outwardly, my rehabilitation seemed to be progressing. I was through with doctors and clinics and bright lights and was going through the motions of my editorial and ecclesi-astical work. In a sense, I was vying for time. I wanted to make no major decisions about my future until I dis-covered what precisely it was that I could and could not do. So this was an interlude, an intermission, a pause. I was trying very hard to follow a normal routine, but that normal routine was interrupted constantly by my anger at people and circumstances that were part of it.

Homeownership became a nightmare. I do not want to overstate my previous ability at home maintenance; before my loss of eyesight it was marginal. I had grown up in parsonages and for ten years had lived in parsonages. In that circumstance when the electricity went out, one called the chairman of the board of trustees—it was the church's property, not mine. But when one forsakes that dubious privilege and becomes an owner of one's own home it is incumbent upon the homeowner to maintain his own property. I used to laugh at the title of Alan King's book, *He Who Owns His Own Home Deserves It,* but I became too angry to laugh at it then. By no stretch of the imagina-tion (not even stretching my habit of exaggeration) was I a handyman. But when I owned a home, like everyone else, I became one.

Margie wanted a dimmer switch replaced on the dining

room light. I put her off, knowing what would happen. But she persisted: "This Saturday *we* will fix the light switch." Now, Margie has many wonderful qualities and attributes, but electrical engineering is not one of them. She hates and fears all things electrical, chemical, and mechanical. I used to say she got confused installing a three-way light bulb. So, I knew it would take my special electrical knowledge to install the rheostat. My own electrical knowledge was only a tad more than an idiot's; on a scale of ten my expertise was about one, but Margie's was zero. "Just tell me what to do," she said, "and I will do it."

There was an immediate breakdown in communication. If I were to ask her if it was a male plug, she would think I was being a male chauvinist—who cares what sex it is! She was certain she would be electrocuted, even though we had cut off the power. I am, of course, an articulate person, but on that day she was deaf and dumb. She could not find what I told her was there; she could not turn what I told her to turn; she could not connect what I told her to connect. What a mess it was! I was not communicating, I was screaming. I was not giving directions to her willing fingers, I was attacking the incompetencies of her personality.

The job did get done. But before I had lost my central vision it would have taken me about three minutes, and I would have been proud when it was finished. Instead, it took a half hour and I was mad when it was done.

What was going on here? It must have been the elephant's touch. I was trying hard to do what I used to do, but I seemed always to be mad about what I did. To be sure, I never was an unflappable automaton; I could get angry once in a while. But I seemed to be often angry: I would mouth off, criticize, and shout at those islands near mine.

Listening to one of my oral tirades over some trivial matter, seven-year-old Ginny asked her mother, "Why is Daddy so angry?" Stupid people! Could they not understand that I was angry not because of them or the trivial instance which had brought on the flare-up? Of course they could not. They could not because the cause was in me. I looked the same as I always did, and for the most part I acted the same as I always did. There was nothing external that was different from what I always had been. But inside my head, behind those wounded eyes, an elephant raged. I cannot do it, he bellowed. I'll never make it.

Like an alcoholic, I knew I was doing terrible things to my family, but I simply could not help myself. They were not to blame; it was not their fault. But was it mine? Had I wanted this to happen to me?

I am not willfully introspective, but I wanted to assign some blame for my internal pain. I thought if I could find some reason for punishment I could endure the punishment. So against my better judgment I asked myself a lot of incriminating questions. Given my religious makeup, the questions turned to God. If at Christmas of 1970 I should be moved to gratitude for my many blessings, then in summer of 1972 when I did not feel blessed I should inquire of the Divinity what went wrong.

One never knows how vulnerable one is to guilt until one suffers an affliction that seeks explanation through reprisal. Unwittingly, I drew up a laundry list of moments in my life in which I had behaved badly. For instance, God gave me skills for parish ministry and called me to the ministry. I had responded with the pledges of ordination but I was no longer a parish minister, I was a journalist. Was God punishing me for having made a change against his will? Or again, every adolescent male of my generation knew that one could go blind from too much sex. I hardly thought that was the case, but oh those masculine fantasies! Or, what about the time I had taken candy from a dime store without paying for it? Remembering one's sordid past does not raise self-esteem. Repentance is healthy, but the search for punitive explanations is not healthy— and it is bad biblical theology.

Those things I believed in my head, but in those days my heart would not stop the search for cause and effect.

I learned to hate and dread some experiences. I hated it when the talk at coffee break in the office turned to the latest books that had been read. I could not participate. I hated it when I encountered an old friend and didn't recognize him because I could not see his face. I dreaded it when the children brought their report cards home—not because they were poor students but because I could not read their grades.

This anger and soul-searching were but part of the story in those days. There were some other wonderful and gracious events happening to me, too. But the trouble with elephants is that they cannot get out of their own skins. They cannot see; they cannot see the real world clearly; they cannot see the love that is still for them and with them.

I had not lost my life, job, or family. Yes, they were in jeopardy, but they had not been taken from me. I was no Job. It did not occur to me at that moment but Saul had lost his sight, and that was part of the conversion of Saul to Paul the apostle. Immediately after his blinding experience he went to the wilderness for forty days. What do you suppose he did there? Maybe he was angry and mournful, maybe he wished he had never thrown stones at the Christians. I did not know what happened to Saul in the desert. All I knew was that this elephant was angry and was not seeing the supportive love of his family, friends, and church.

They did not know what to say or do, so they went on about their business of doing what they had always done. Their world had not changed because mine had. I was in danger of screwing up their world for them.

It did not become real or clear to me until some time later, but even in this time of desperation I was the beneficiary of some powerful help. My children do not love me for my eyes. They accepted with remarkable equanimity that I no longer played catch after school, that I could not see them in a play at school, that Mom had to drive the family where they wanted to go. My friends at church wanted to speak to me, but what was there to say to me? I did not initiate conversation so they ignored what had happened. That made me think they had forgotten and were going on their merry ways. And as for God, that great benefactor of my life to whom I had been thankful, that God at that very moment of desperation was offering help and hope to me. The psalmist said something about the "valley of the shadow of death"—that is where I was, in shadow and experiencing a kind of death—and he went on to say, "Thy rod and thy staff they comfort me." There was a rod and a staff there, but I could not grasp them.

An angry elephant alone on an island feels very sorry for himself.

Trying Harder

I had never realized how many people practice medicine. I do not mean the roster of the AMA, or even the quacks outside the pale of the disciplines of medical science. What I was discovering was that my relatives, friends, even strangers wanted me to try their remedies.

I received a note from a lovely lady who had known me when I was in high school. She had heard of my affliction and had sent me details of a foot massage technique supposedly sure to restore vision. She had done it all her life, and she was ninety-two. I shuddered whenever Kathryn Kuhlman was within two hundred miles of Chicago: Invitations to attend one of her faith healing meetings would flood in. A stranger saw me fumbling around in a public place, discerned my malady, and offered his prescription: a trip to the Philippines for psychic surgery. My parents sent me a forty-year supply of vitamin E—"Adelle Davis uses these and you know how well she sees!" I took them for a couple of weeks to remind myself that at age thirty-eight I was still an obedient child, and because I knew they were sent in love.

By far the most persistent remedy advanced was an eye transplant. This solution emerges in the American mentality as residue from the Industrial Revolution. We are still convinced of the practicality of interchangeable parts: If a part—metal or tissue—is defective, get another. I am a product of my society, too, and so I asked Dr. Hackett about an eye transplant. He went to some length in explaining why there was no such thing. Corneas, a relatively small portion of the eye, can be transplanted with efficacy in some cases. My diseased tissue is in the back of my eye, amid a network of millions of nerve cells. There is no way to sever and reconnect that network. The eyes would stay as they were. Leave interchangeable parts to automobiles and rifles.

The truth is that at that point I welcomed all those medicinal testimonies and listened eagerly to each piece of advice. I was not aware of it at the time, but in retrospect two powerful forces were loose in my life. I would not be "cured" until I had come to grips with those two forces.

The first of those was my vulnerability. I was openly, nakedly, obviously hurting. I was in a state of panic and desperation. I would entertain even the most patently outlandish suggestions. This was not a rational time, it was emotional. My loss was very painful. If Mephistopheles had made me any kind of proposition, I would have taken it. Yes, I would have sold my soul for the promise of a return of normal vision. Fortunately for me, I was dealing only with well-wishers. Others—even strangers—wanted to see me helped, and that was therapeutically good in itself. Had I encountered the unscrupulous it would have been bad. This may be why doctors are shy about rehabilitation resources. They could spend a major portion of their professional lives—as I would subsequently do—just sorting out the competent helpers from the charlatans. Anyone who hurts is vulnerable. I grieved for my loss and was vulnerable to promises of restoration.

The second reason I was susceptible at that stage was more profound. I was in the first stage of grief, called shock and denial. I could not believe that my eyes were "permanently, irreparably, and irrevocably" damaged. I could believe it in my head—Dr. Gass knew what the evidence was. I could tell every time I looked at anything. It was there. But I did not live in my head, I lived in what Christians call "the heart." There was a center of being that was me, and that is where the warfare raged. It was my heart that refused to accept the verdict. I was denying the truth. It was unpleasant and painful. I preferred to look for resurrection rather than accept death. In my heart I could not believe what had happened to me. Surely it was a bad dream and I would awaken. Surely there was a cure out there that would heal my hurt in here.

I could not be healed until I accepted the finality of the facts.

While I spoke with Dr. Hackett of cures, he mentioned several other avenues of interest. They were not so much cures as small coping instruments. He suggested that I talk to the Chicago Lighthouse for the Blind, a fine, philanthropic institution. However, I did not follow this avenue. I did not for two reasons, one of which was right and one of which was dead wrong. The right reason was that I was not blind: I was partially sighted. I did not need lead dogs or white canes, and I certainly did not want to manage a newsstand. Those things the Lighthouse for the Blind does, and God bless them for that. The totally blind need that; I did not. Incidentally, this began to emerge as a major theme for me: Our society is responsive to the special needs of the totally blind, and it should be. But the groupies with anxious faces in the halls of opthalmological wards are not all blind; many are visually imperfect. Where do they go? Where would I go? The second reason I did not then take his advice was my heart problem. I really did not want to admit that this was final. I still hoped deeply, in the recesses of my being, that this was temporary. Something would set it right yet. If I were to go for rehabilitation it would mean permanency, and I was not ready to accept that yet. Sorry, Doc, but I will stay away from the Chicago Lighthouse for the Blind.

Hackett's second proposal was simpler and more acceptable. He handed me a sheet of paper on his stationery. It read, "This is to certify that Robert G. Kemper is legally blind." There was a starkness to the words that pained me, but as we talked my pain was soothed by dollars. He told me the emphasis in the letter was upon "legally" and not "blind." I learned that legal blindness is a term concocted by lawyers and the courts. It does not mean total blindness. In simple terms it means I cannot read the largest letter on the doctor's eye chart. This piece of paper was good for $600 a year—i.e., it would be one more exemption on my income tax. At last, a small reward for my affliction. What I subsequently discovered was that the special costs to me in dollars, not to mention psychic inconvenience, far exceeded the exemption. But even in pain my head was turned by money. I took the letter and filed it with my income tax.

Hackett's third suggestion had to do with welfare. He was virtually ignorant of the pertinent facts—that would be another full-time occupation for doctors. But the point was that I should explore what I might receive. I had internal difficulties in accepting his advice on this one. Again, it would mean admitting a permanency that inwardly I was denying. But, on the other hand, how long could Alan keep me on, and how long could Joan keep covering for me? I had to think of these financial matters.

My college friend, Dick Kowal, stepped in to help me out. I was a problem for Dick. On the one hand we were friends from college and neighbors in Western Springs; on the other hand, he was my insurance agent—specifically, the carrier of my group medical insurance policy. And

wasn't there a permanent disability clause in that policy?
It could be an expense to the company for a young buck
like me. I genuinely believe that Dick stepped in to help me
out from friendship and not insurance considerations.
Anyway, he took me to our district Social Security office.

This proved to be another of those new discoveries that
would affect my future interests, viz., the unresponsive-
ness of bureaucracy to human need. There are miles of red
tape involved in dealings with the administrators of socie-
tal largesse. I will spare you the details of triplicate copies
and go to the point: I had come upon a "catch-22" situation. If I were unable to work because of my visual disability, I would be kept by the government in a manner to
which I was not accustomed. They would pay me about
$400 a month until my children reached the age of eight-
een. That sum would hardly pay my house mortgage! But
the "catch-22" was that should I try to work, even falter-
ingly, I would be entitled to absolutely zero. I am sure
there is a wisdom to that policy, but it is buried in the
minds of the bureaucratic conceivers. If I were to give up
altogether I would be subsidized, but if I tried to make it
on my own I would be entitled to nothing. There is no
middle ground here. Kowal exclaimed to the clerk, "But
this man is an editor! Surely you can imagine his difficulty
in working in that capacity, but he wants to try even on a
reduced basis." She was unimpressed with my particular
circumstances—her job was not to reason why, but to file
until the day she died. I think the Social Security Adminis-
tration is weird and wrong.

There was one other big reason for not accepting all the
helpful advice I received from (it seemed) the whole world:
I had my own plan. It was conceived on the plane back
from Miami, and I lived it during subsequent months. It
was a futile plan, but at the time it seemed like a good

idea. Just as the Industrial Revolution made us hospitable to the idea of interchangeable parts, so too the American culture makes us hospitable to the idea of individual effort. That was my great plan: I would try harder. Yes, I had this problem, but I would not let it undo me. I would rise above it. How? By sheer dint of human effort. If I had to work at editing twenty hours a day instead of ten, I would do it. But, by God, I would win this battle!

I will not disparage this plan altogether. It served me well. I worked harder and longer than I would have had to without this problem. A domesticated elephant becomes a great beast of burden. To this day everything I do takes me longer than it would a normally sighted person. Extra work time is the lot of the partially sighted person.

But, ultimately, effort is not the solution. If effort is one's only strategy, what will you do when you come against situations that cannot be budged even by inordinate, superhuman effort? You will bat your head against the immovable object. I know, I have done it. The real reason my massive effort strategy was the wrong one was that it did not confront the real problem. Just as doctors struggle to name a disease so they finally can begin to control and affect it, so too did my problem need to be rightly named before I could deal with it. If my problem was blindness, then effort might be the best solution. But if my problem was the pain of loss, then effort alone would not do it.

But I was months away from baptizing it with the right name, and in the meantime could only try harder. And I grew steadily more angry and frustrated because I simply could not win this battle by effort alone.

Before an elephant can begin to dance, he must understand what he needs to be able to dance.

Not driving was a symbol of something larger with

which I struggled constantly. It meant dependency. When I want to go anywhere—live free, extend my range—I am dependent upon someone else. That is an awful estate for a young American male. From our earliest days we are programmed to "stand on our own two feet." That is probably a good thing, but if I were to do that I would just stand in one place and never go anywhere. Grudgingly, I had to accept dependency and ask people to take me places—at their convenience, of course. (Darn it!)

The acceptance of dependency posed a problem in addition to representing a step toward rehabilitation. I was tempted to play the game of dependency all out. If I wanted to—and sometimes I did—I could be virtually helpless and let everybody else do my bidding. I was close to that status on the magazine: Joan did my work there. Margie could become my servant, not my wife.

It is a very thin line between a dependency that encourages slavery and a dependency that recognizes the facts of one's limitations.

There are some oddities and some positive fallout from the mobility problem. It is paradoxical, for instance, but quite true, that I can go by myself from coast to coast on an airplane more easily than I can go to the suburb adjacent to our home. The difference is public transportation versus private.

The coast-to-coast possibilities were a happy development for me. In February 1972 I returned to Claremont, California, to have a follow-up conversation with Peter Drucker, whom I had interviewed the year before. The prospect of accomplishment had urged me to overcome the fears of travel without normal vision. I was surprised at how easily it went. Bus to plane, cab to hotel, feet to interview, and then retrace. Easy. There were some hitches. Airlines post their flight departures on small, remote signs. Looking at the board, I asked the person standing next to me where my flight was to depart. He never looked at me, just read what I wanted to know. People are terrific if you ask for help when you need it. I have never been refused information when I ask for it. So I returned from California with two hours of taped conversation for Joan to type; I would tell her how to edit it. Hey, is that elephant really trying to dance?

On the positive side of not driving, Margie had a big breakthrough. Having always been economically marginal, we have had only one car. And who had the claim on that chariot to freedom? Why, the lord and master of the house, of course. If he could not use it, then she could. But that has become a permanent fact of life and not an occasional indulgence. Margie thrives on her freedom and range of mobility. It has been good for her.

At first, when she drove me anywhere one could count on an argument between us. I claimed she was lousy at directions, which was demonstrably true—she was. I would fly into a rage at her ineptitude in missing turns off expressways. I screamed at her—like a wounded elephant, shall I say?—when she would screw up the sensible itinerary. But I knew, and think she did too, that the issue was not navigation. It was my longing to be behind that wheel, to be in command, to take charge. I really am an acculturated American, aren't I?

Elephants make lousy backseat drivers. They hurt when not behind the wheel.

Some Technological Wonders

One never knows where help will come from. A great discovery was made for me, and I never would have expected its source.

Margie's mother died some years ago, and her father had remarried. His wife, my stepmother-in-law, is Betty Klontz, who has a married daughter living in California. (Bear with this genealogical digression; it is relevant to the surprise.)

Betty had flown to California to visit Marilyn, and while she was there the two ladies went to the beauty shop. Under the windy whirl of the dryer, Marilyn browsed through an old *Reader's Digest*. (Pretty exciting story so far, right?) She finished first and made small talk while her mother was coiffured. Marilyn mentioned an article from this old *Reader's Digest*—about a man who invented a machine to help him see better. Betty asked to see the article. It was entitled, "Sam Geniski's Marvelous Machine." Betty scanned it and thought of me. In her resourcefulness she pilfered the magazine from the shop and stuffed it into her handbag to bring back to Chicago.

It was a good article, about a man born blind in one eye and with 10 percent vision in the other. (He had my attention right away.) Despite that handicap he went on to get a Ph.D. in physics. (He also had my admiration.) He had done his university work by means of a closed-circuit television receiver. (And he had my future in his seeing machine.)

Bless the editors of the *Reader's Digest:* They included addresses for further information. I wrote for it, but remained skeptical. Television is for entertainment, not work.

The answers came back with an invitation to see a demonstration. Where? The Chicago Lighthouse for the Blind. Must I still go through the white-cane-and-lead-dog bit? "No," they said, "come in for a demonstration." Margie drove me to their office downtown, where a pleasant young woman greeted me and ushered me into a small room. A television set was on the table, a black object to the right of it. The young lady turned switches and twisted knobs. She invited me to sit behind the television screen as she reached for a newspaper.

I will never forget that great day. For the first time in eighteen months I read a newspaper with my own eyes! The elephant did a pirouette right there, in that little room, in front of the television screen.

Sam's seeing machine worked for me. You place what you want to read on a movable table. A spotlight shines on the paper, with a mirror above receiving the signals for the illuminated area. A small television camera with a large lens focuses on the mirror and plays the image through the television screen, but forty times larger. A line of newspaper type will appear on the screen in letters up to three inches high. The print is big enough to read with the peripheral vision I have left. You move the table left to right and up and down with your hand. It takes practice, but when an elephant really wants to learn the ballet, he can learn anything!

To read again—what I want, when I want, how I

want—this was too good to be true. But there was even more. The lady showed me how to add a column of figures. I could keep my own checkbook! She showed me how I could learn to write in my own hand. I would have to look elsewhere (at the screen) and let my hand (off to the right) make its marks, but do you know what that meant? I could edit manuscripts! O elephant, do an arabesque!

There was more yet to come! The lady suggested that I come back another time to go through their low vision clinic. She pulled out a pair of glasses that might help me, and only then did I realize she was me—I mean, one of my group, partially sighted. I had not noticed it. The glasses interested me too. They were not as good as the television but one could carry them more easily.

I subsequently procured a pair of glasses from their low visual aids department. They were weird-looking, and they made me look weird when using them. But I was far enough into the rehabilitation struggle that vanity was diminishing, and I did not much care what I looked like as long as I could try hard to overcome. The glasses have one large magnifying lens on the left side—only one, because I would have my old companion, double vision, if there were two. The physics of optics has not much changed since Galileo stated their principles. To make an object magnify to the beholder, a convex lens is used and the focal length shortened. Therefore, you hold something to be read right up to your nose—and I mean to the nose: You get ink on your nose, it's that close! The glasses can be used only for reading, not for seeing beyond one's nose.

Thus was created the elephant's reading ballet. I am still a lousy reader—slow, limited, and halting. But at least I am reading!

Short-Term Problems, Long-Term Possibilities

Wounds have a way of widening. When one hurts inside, all other changes and departures from the norm are perceived as threats and further pain. I had to deal with two of those. At the time of their confrontation they seemed awesome mountains, but proved to be passages to the other side of the mountains.

A century before, when I was seeing normally, I had been invited and had accepted an invitation to address the Ohio Pastors' Convention in Columbus. It was a big deal, with thousands of clergy, and an honor to be asked to speak there. But when the time came I did not want to do it.

Joan argued I must, I could: "There is nothing wrong with your head or tongue." I knew that, but I had spent twenty years learning how to be an effective public speaker, and the way I did that was to write out my speeches. I would write once to get the basic ideas on paper, and a second time to stylize the ideas into prose, with well-turned sentences. Modesty aside, I was good at it. I had become a rising young orator of considerable appeal and effect. All that really means is that I had worked very hard to learn a craft that was important to me.

The problem I confronted is simply stated: If I could not read my speech, I could not speak effectively.

"Nonsense," said Joan. "Nonsense," claimed Marge. Easy for them to say—they did not have to stand in front of an audience and invite their attention. They did not remember the horror of Reformation Sunday in Springfield. I would have to make the speech, and I remembered the horror of not seeing my words.

There was much prestige and a handsome fee associated with this address. Did I say vanity was dead? No, just diminished, not dead. From very unclear and mixed motives, I prepared to deliver the address.

It was expected to be an hour long, on a subject I knew a lot about: the agenda of the ministerial profession. The preparation for this speech began a pattern and a discipline that I follow to this day. First, I think. I sit and stare into space, just thinking of what needs to be said and how to say it. Second, I talk into a tape recorder, saying words and phrases from my thoughts. One can stop, erase, and restate on a tape similar to erasing words on a typewriter. When I am reasonably satisfied with the tape I listen to it over and over and over. I grow sick of hearing my own voice. But the words, sequence, and sections become etched on my inner ear. I become a human tape recorder: Push the button, and I play back. As I listen to the tape I may write an occasional big word on a single piece of paper. These are my "notes." They really are not because I still cannot see them clearly. In truth, they are my security blanket, for if I go blank and panic I cannot grab the page and figure out what that one word means.

That is how I got ready for Columbus. Margie went with me. She might have to pick up the pieces and carry me home in a paper bag. I was really scared. "Relax," she told me. "If you forget your next point, just hold up one of those pages and let the audience tell you where you are!" What a sense of humor she has. But then she did not have to remember the 9,000 words I would need for the next hour.

I did it. No, I did it well. And I did it well by objective standards. I didn't forget a thing—it flowed with grace and power. I did it! By subjective standards, knowing my precedent anxiety and difficulties, I did a magnificent job. I could again speak in public if I worked hard at it. The elephant twirled off the stage to generous applause.

As a matter of fact, the speech was so good that I subsequently gave it about a hundred times more, all over the country. It became known as "The Speech" at the office. Each time I just listened again to the tape, carrying my security blanket with me to the rostrum. I was delighted at this development, but it was one thing to memorize one speech, something else to do different ones on different occasions.

The second mountain I had to confront was larger. Joan was leaving, and the finances of the situation would not permit her replacement. I was the one who ought to have gone, but I could not let go. We had become a good editorial team. I supplied the decisions that must be made about the magazine, and she supplied the labor of editing manuscripts, proofing galleys, cutting and pasting, and authorizing page layouts. But she had decided to leave, and Alan had to consider canceling the magazine.

I urged him to let me keep it going for a while, with me hiring people to help me as needed. It was August, and we agreed to try it through December.

The ride from Western Springs to Chicago had become a drudge since I could not read on the bumpy train. Furthermore, my reading machine was in Western Springs, and I needed its use to edit manuscripts. There was a necessary solution: Move my office to Western Springs. It would save commuting time and give me the use of the television system, both so I could try harder. God, this was a determined elephant!

Western Springs is a lovely residential village. There is little office space, and it is expensive. My house was too small. Where should I go? I had an idea, but it would take a lot of doing.

My good friends, Chuck and Marge Klindera, were very supportive through this whole ugly time. They had even driven to Columbus with Margie and me to hear the great unveiling of The Speech. Besides being very supportive, Chuck has two other attributes that proved essential to this phase of rehabilitation: He is an architect by profession and was chairman of the board of trustees of the church, where both of us are members. I put the idea to him, and he agreed to see what could be done.

Chuck was terrific! He not only won the approval of the trustees to rent space in the church building to me, but he also agreed to design and build an office. It was a wonderful stroke of luck—or was it Providence coming back into my life?

I needed a special kind of office, with lots of room for all the gear I had accumulated as an editor and television watcher. Furthermore, I had developed an interesting avocation. Before my eye problems began (was this, too, that good Providence?) I had become interested in a new communication medium: prerecorded cassette tapes. I had formed my own small business, Telepax, to record lectures, sermons, etc., for sale to clergy. So I needed a recording studio in my office too. Good friend that he is, Chuck designed and built a wonderful place for me in a little-used third-floor room of the large church building.

Because of that office and its recording facilities some other friends, Al Williams and John Muir, made me a business proposition. Would I become a communications consultant for the Illinois Conference of the United Church of Christ? The Conference is the ecclesiastical equivalent of a diocese and serves churches of that denomination throughout Illinois. We agreed to produce information tapes for the churches and to advise the judicatory about this communications process. I did not do them much good, but I liked them and the work very much. Perhaps they hired me for their personal mission because they knew well my struggle. For whatever reason, it pleased me.

I was beginning to feel useful again. Two years after the onset of the disease and one year after my resolve to really try hard to overcome, I was getting it together again.

I was editing the magazine by myself—sort of. Doug Runnels, a seminary student, had been hired to edit some of the manuscripts on a free-lance basis. Margie was learning the printing business. When press time came she and our friend Peggy Taylor would trek up to the third floor of the church with paste and scissors and my directions to lay out the pages of the magazine for the printer to follow.

There I was, on the third floor of the First Congregational Church of Western Springs—legally blind, but editing a magazine, operating a business, and consulting. Not bad. This elephant, by sheer effort—and the help of a lot of wonderful people—was doing the ballet.

Was there anything he could not do? Yes.

A Great Chance, and a Refusal

The First Congregational Church is a central character in this story. It had already touched my life twice and was about to touch it again. Let me tell you more about this church.

It is a large, distinguished church with beautiful, spacious buildings and a rich heritage of leadership in our village and denomination. It has had a large congregation since the 1950s; there are about 1,500 members and three ministers. The congregation has some wonderful, talented, religious people, and it positively affects the lives of many people, including mine.

When I first met the congregation in 1959 as a twenty-four-year-old seminarian, Edward Manthei was senior minister—a giant of a person, preacher, and pastor. I had been receiving a wonderfully rich academic education at the University of Chicago, but it was rivaled by the one year of wonderfully rich apprenticeship I had with this church and great teacher. Margie was teaching public school, and I played minister in the church. The people could not have been nicer to me. They knew one had to begin somewhere, and they took me green and helped me mature.

After ten years of pastorates in Ohio and New Jersey the opportunity came to work for *The Christian Century* and move back to the Chicago area. It was Ken Seim, senior minister at the time, and a group of laypersons who kept their eyes open for a house. After several false starts another parishioner, Myron Ash, found us a house in the village. We were "back home" among the friends we had made ten years earlier in this very church.

When I speak of supportive friends during the descendency of my eye disease and the ascendency of my rehabilitation, with only a few exceptions they were the friends in the fellowship of this church. They really cared for me and my family during that up-and-down period, and the use of space in the building for my office was a visible and powerful symbol of their constant good care.

So, twice they had touched me: once to teach me the craft of ministry, and then to care for me in my affliction and attempt at rehabilitation. There are deep ties and helpful hands in that congregation.

But in 1973 the congregation that has meant so much to me posed a horrendous dilemma.

It had an innocuous beginning, then became wretched. Ken Seim announced his plan to retire, and the congregation, as customary in this denomination, appointed a search committee to secure a replacement. Ken had given a year's notice to allow ample time for search and discovery. I wanted to be on that committee. After all, I am a clergyman, know a lot of other clergy, and more important, I could offer a little repayment to the church by volunteering my special connections. I was passed over, but was assured the elected committee would use me as a consultant, which they did.

In free church polity (congregationalism) the selection of a minister is a painstaking, frustrating chore. The committee must design a profile of the congregation's needs and then find a candidate whose contours reasonably match them. It is not a precise science, and the bigger the church the more quirks in the profile. They went on and on at their task. I helped out a couple of times, but they did not find my particular suggestions productive. Time moved on. A decision had not been made, and Ken Seim left. The church was without a senior minister.

After all they had done for me I felt I really should offer some help at this critical juncture. I mentioned it to Bill Reace, the moderator and a good friend, and his response was to ask, "How would you like to preach for us during the interim?" "Gee, thanks, Bill," I said, "but I don't think I could do that. My eyes, you know. To make one speech is one thing, to make a series of different sermons is something else. Anything but that. I simply could not do it. This interim could go on for months. I am not able to preach for a month of Sundays."

I honestly am not sure why, but I called Bill back and assented. Maybe I saw that as a chance to pay back my debt to the congregation. Maybe I wanted to try preaching once more. Maybe I accepted because it had a terminus. Maybe it was a tug of God I did not understand. I agreed to preach for two months.

Suddenly, unexpectedly, people were swarming to church on Sunday morning. What was bringing them? Hometown boy? Curiosity about elephants? A supportive congregation in a time of church crisis? I didn't know what to make of it. But two facts were unassailable: They came, and I was preaching again.

The interim agreement ended. I felt good about what I had done, but other duties demanded my primary attention—mainly, working my tail off at doing my ballet.

Our wonderful chairman of the search committee, Jim Berry, asked to see me and I expected to consult again. Instead, he had come to report that the committee, at the urging of the congregation, had authorized him to sound me out about a candidacy. Would I consider standing as a candidate for the position of senior minister? I was stunned, and promised I would let him know.

Margie and I began talking and talking and talking. What of the magazine? What of Telepax? What of having to preach every Sunday? What of not driving? What of weddings, funerals, baptisms? I simply could not manage it. Besides, I was sure they felt sorry for me. And I was managing well the things I was doing, as well as I could ever expect things to be.

I told Jim I was honored and flattered (which was true), but that I could not offer myself as a candidate because of my commitment to the magazine (which was true and not true). Please tell the committee and the congregation, "Thanks, but no thanks."

I felt really good to be asked, but really bad about saying no. The congregation needed something more than an elephant who could do a ballet for a couple of Sundays. The matter was closed. My mind was made up.

Getting to the Heart of the Matter

All that time I had been playing a game. It was good that I was winning the game—but I was playing the wrong game.

My mind was not clear. Usually, when I make a decision I begin to live it and put the precedent ambiguities aside. But this time I could not be rid of them. Why had I told Jim no? What was the real reason?

The party line was clear and reasonable. I was the founding editor of an important magazine. It would fold if I left it. I had had some hard times, certainly, but I had worked very hard and had come back a long way. I was sure I could keep on keeping on.

That line was challenged by what I also knew to be true. I was a minister, not a journalist. I owed this congregation a great deal. By taking this position I would be copping out on my plan to overcome by sheer effort—I would be giving up, admitting I could not make it as a blind editor.

But, said a third voice to the pro-and-con dialogue, they want you. This is a congregation of free people. They do not have to take anything or anybody. They made up their own minds, and they wanted me. Why did I not want them? That was the dilemma.

I talked and talked and talked. To Margie. To Ed Manthei. To Ken Seim. To anyone who would listen. I told the pros, cons, and in-betweens. I became a real bore, an elephant who could not make up his mind. I grew sick and tired of all the ambiguities.

And then a new thought churned up in the mix of these arguments. From somewhere it grew and grew in my consciousness until it had to be dealt with. I had not refused because of editorial commitments: I had said no because I feared failure.

I had said no because of self-image. I had really believed all the business about elephants doing ballet. I had really thought the problem was learning to function again—the reason I was working so hard.

My whole game plan had been hanging on not giving up. But why? *Because I would not admit what had happened.* All that time I had struggled to make everything go on as if nothing had happened. I had refused to admit that I, the "rising young man," was blind—permanently, irreparably, irrevocably. I had suffered a loss. It would not be restored no matter what I did. I could probably continue to play the game and win, in a way, but it was ultimately the wrong game and ultimately I would not win.

I had told the congregation no because I had not yet confronted the truth. I did not need help with my eyes—I had that. I did not need more effort to make the loss less powerful in my life—I had done that. I needed healing, forgiveness. I needed grace. And I needed God.

The old, religious language to tell of this churning is the only one that will do. I have known the words from my youth—like Job, I "heard of thee with my ear, but now I see thee face to face." I would not be healed by effort. I could be healed by grace. I had to discover that my life, even in its affliction, was in God's hands, not mine. I could not save myself. All that effort was an attempt to heal myself. I could not forgive myself for what had happened to me, to those I love and work with. I had made a mess of things. Perhaps I could not explain my tragic flaw that had brought this awful thing upon me, but I had been punished for my wrongs. And as Dr. Gass had said, I would "learn to live with it."

What a fool I had been. I had made it a win/lose situation. I had made myself into something I wasn't. I was handicapped in the spirit, not in the eyes. I had allowed myself to become an elephant and had indulged myself in thinking the lousy ballet was my accomplishment. It was my curse, because I had made it so.

I had run away from the sources of life that were for me, self-indulgently licking my wounds and playing the part of helpless victim even in my achievements. I wanted to be loved for something I wasn't, an unfortunate victim of circumstance. I could not accept the love that was given me for what I was and not for what I was not. I had made a cage of my problem, and what was worse, had grown comfortable in it.

What a big dummy. All the time I had been loved. All the time I had been free. All the time I had been healed. And I had not had the sense to discover it, trust it, and live it. The elephant did the ballet rather than admit that his broken heart was being healed by grace.

The healing I had sought was at hand all the time. I had not accepted it, but it was there. God does not punish anyone, we punish ourselves. God wants all to be whole. Those forces are there before the first cell division in a mother's womb.

The forgiveness I had sought was always there, I just would not face my own anger. I was hostile to doctors, to presenters of cures, and most of all to myself. I had thought if I were any kind of a man at all I would master the loss. Fool. I had never forgiven myself, not once.

The grace I had sought had always been there. Luther was right: Man cannot save himself by works. What I had prized as independence was faintly masked pride. I had wanted to work everything out for myself, trusting no one but me. No wonder I could not let go of my blind carcass: It was a proud possession.

O God, could I trust you?

That was my hope.

I phoned Jim Berry: "Jim, if it is not too late can I reconsider your invitation?"

The rest was grace.

WHAT DANCING ELEPHANTS KNOW

But that is the beginning
of a new story—
the story of
the gradual renewal of a man,
the story of his gradual
regeneration, of his passing
from one world into another, of
his initiation into a new
unknown life.

—Fyodor Dostoyevsky/*Crime and Punishment*

The Next Story

You know of my loss, as truthfully and accurately as I could tell it, and of the year in my life in which I learned to dance, to function with a visual handicap, to rehabilitate myself by enormous effort and determination. The chronology ended with a new discovery—that in the process of losing my central eyesight and struggling to recover I fell victim to another disease, this time a disease of the spirit, not the body: a loss of self-worth, a box of limitations that convinced me I could not function again as a parish minister. The discovery of this debilitating victimization was met by another discovery, the presence of grace in the midst of life and loss.

As Dostoyevsky had said, whenever one story ends another begins. My response to the first—renewal, redemption—becomes a new story. What happened to me was a landmark, an ending. It affected me in such a way that I will never be the same again. A change has occurred with absolute lasting power. I can speculate what may have been had I not experienced the loss, but the unassailable fact of the present and the inevitable fact of the future is that it did happen to me, and it has made an irreversible difference.

I am writing these words more than five years after that day in December of 1970, and since that fateful moment in the Senate gallery my whole life has taken another course, a surprising, vexing new direction. The truth is that at this point I do not think much about what has happened to me. The surprising factor is that its constancy—every time I look at anything I am consciously aware of the absence of normal vision—makes it comfortable for me. If I were to have days of normal vision and days of visual loss, that would be unbearable. But the fact that it is permanent, irreparable, and irreversible, dread words when I first heard them, makes it now manageable. When finality is accepted, one begins to cope with the resulting disorders. When one copes long enough, a new order begins. With the passage of time the new order becomes normalcy.

That shift from complaint over what has happened to coping with what has happened is a wonderful personal experience. Unfortunately, it is personal and not social. The totally blind person encounters enormous prejudice by society, as society knows best the horrors of the loss and not the wonders of resurrection. The partially sighted person encounters a different, more insidious, prejudice. In the case of a person who sees everything in general but nothing in particular, one's fellow human beings feel deceived. Others know of my visual loss, but when they hear that I play golf (no matter how ineptly) or that I function as senior minister of a large congregation, they are surprised and confused over their expectations of who I am and what I can or cannot do. A major theme in my new life story is surprising people by confronting their own expectations of visually handicapped people and exposing the losses with which they too live.

The subject of this story has no end. It begins with the acceptance of loss as a fact and goes on with the ways in which one lives with that loss, exploring the ways in which grace is a powerful presence in all of life. Freedom—personal, internal freedom—is the subject of the continuing story. The loss I experienced was physical. It affected my life and work in a demonstrable way. But in the wake of that physical loss and the effort to overcome it, I sacrificed a more precious gift: the internal me that makes me who I am and not just an elephant. The sadness in my heart these days is caused not by my loss of eyesight but rather by the pain others suffer when they fall victim to their circumstances and sacrifice their inner freedom in the false hope that they will prevail against their lot in life.

The in word of my generation is *liberation*. It has enormous power for many of this time and place. It is the hope for those who are oppressed, not only by racial, economic, or sexual circumstances. This story is about personal liberation, from the circumstances of my very own life. My impression, looking around me, is that this imprisonment is familiar to us all. We make ourselves prisoners of ourselves. Who we think we are has mightily affected how we live—as I discovered. So this story of liberation is about the assertion of personal freedom in the midst of adverse circumstances and the possibilities of trust—which is the life of grace.

The Call Comes

The pastoral search committee, at the urging of the congregation, had once before offered me the opportunity to be their candidate to the congregation, and I had refused. I know now that I refused because of my spiritual pain. I had surrendered my inner freedom to my physical condition. I thought I could not do what would be required of me. I was sure I would be a problem to the church and an embarrassment to them. Further, I was sure that sightless, I had nothing to offer this very challenging congregation.

When I let it be known that I wanted to be considered a candidate, to the everlasting credit of that fine group of people they did not fall at my feet and say, "Praise the Lord!" Instead, they looked me straight on and said, "How come? How does it happen, Brother Kemper, that just a few months ago you could not be moved and now you come for our approval?" It was a very sensible question to ask. It was also one for which I had a not very sensible answer.

The truth was that in the interval some important healings and changes in my spirit had happened. But I could not speak of it then and could not explain the changes to them, maybe because I could not explain them to myself. The result was fortunate: They made me go through the same rigorous process they had designed for all of the candidates. Their immediate decision was not to select me as their candidate, but to let me stand before them as a potential candidate. In itself that was a high compliment and could have been taken as a vote of confidence: I was to be treated like anybody else! They probably did not know it at the time, but that was very reassuring to me. Why? Because I still thought I was different, an elephant who would amuse and amaze by his faltering efforts to dance. They were *not* feeling sorry for me. What they were saying was, "We do not want to see an elephant do the ballet. We want to see the stuff of a religious leader. Forget the ballet nonsense, forget the eyesight question. What do you think this church is and should become?" Wow, what an attitude!

So we went through the whole rigorous agenda of the selection process. What were my beliefs, my professional experiences, my competencies, my weaknesses? What did I think and would I do about preaching, Christian education, youth work, pastoral care, church management? It was an exhausting and exhilarating process. For several nights over several weeks we talked and talked. The subject of eyesight never arose.

Finally, one night George Norton asked me, "Bob, how will you conduct a funeral service?" There was a long pause—on my part and theirs. They had heard me preach, they knew I could speak without notes. But all the emotions of faith and fear of death cluster around that very special ministry. How would I handle that moment? My response was not an answer. I asked, "George, would you trust me to conduct your funeral service?" A short pause. "Yes," he said, "I would." That became the tone of the subsequent conversation: Would we trust each other in the ministries of this church that we shared? That question really was the symbol of the moment for me, and I think for them. My growing edge was hoping that the grace of God would enable me to live and minister. Theirs was the discovery that the grace of God can be trusted in those long, arduous processes of church life. The conclusion of the negotiations was only the inauguration of the larger congregational process: Could we trust each other and, more importantly, could we trust the grace of God to mutually bless and direct our life together?

It was a great day in June of 1973. Following the practice of this denomination the pastoral search committee submitted my name to the congregation for election as senior minister. Margie and I and the three children were sequestered at the home of Eleanor and Bill Reace for the vote, waiting for the phone call. I was not nervous, I had an unfamiliar calm. I just knew it would be good. The phone rang, and the vote was affirmative. Would we all come to the church and greet the congregation?

The whole congregation was assembled in the sanctuary, singing as they awaited our arrival. As we came in they had begun to sing, "Blest be the Tie That Binds." I had known it from my earliest days and joined with my family and the congregation in lusty singing.

I was carrying my working Bible—not only is the Holy Bible the authority of faith for the congregation, it is also the preacher's tool. Clergy accumulate dozens of them: different editions, translations, resources. But usually there is one they use more than others, and that was the one I was carrying. It was a powerful symbol. This particular Bible had been a gift to me, thirteen years earlier—by this congregation. I spoke aloud the names of the signatories on the frontispiece. Some former leaders were gone; the other signatories were seated before me in the pews of that very sanctuary. I was home again.

In the pages of that Bible was tucked a card, always kept there, containing a biblical verse: "I will set shepherds over them who will care for them, and they shall fear no more, nor be dismayed, neither shall any be missing, says the Lord" (Jer. 23:4). It had been given to me, as was customary, by the president of the Chicago Theological Seminary on the day I graduated. He saw a future for me as a pastor, a shepherd, and hence that particular passage. I was not only home, I was back at my vocation again.

Tears were in the eyes of my wife and children, moved by the public recognition I was receiving. Tears were in the eyes of many in the congregation, sensing a new development and direction for their much-loved church. Tears were in my eyes too, for all those reasons, but also because of the awesome awareness within me of the power of grace. The grace of God had delivered us to that moment of ending and of beginning. The tears were embarrassing to no one. They opened us to receive the hugs and handshakes of the ties that bind us.

I stood in the warmth of that congregation as their preacher, pastor, teacher, counselor, leader, and most important, friend. I did not stand there as the amazing blind man, the elephant who danced, the unfortunate victim of disease, the object of their pity. I stood in that place as person and pastor, and it was good to stand in that way because of the saving power of grace.

It is one thing—a great experience—to be called as senior minister by a congregation; it is something else again to perform the functions of the office on a day-to-day basis. I have had to learn to do the public acts of ministry in new ways.

How Does He Do It?

It now seems to me ordinary rather than astonishing or noteworthy that while legally blind I manage my professional life with a measure of competency. The reason is simple: I have done what I do long enough that it has become natural to me. But you may want to know the specific adjustments I have made to compensate for my visual deprivation.

Were you to attend worship here on a typical Sunday it is unlikely you would notice anything particularly unusual. I am reasonably sure, because persons who visit our congregation are later dumbfounded to learn I am legally blind. That pleases me. I am also very pleased when my parishioners forget, and that is the highest compliment they continue to pay me: by treating me as a normally sighted person.

If you came to our worship service looking for telltale signs, they are there. I never read any part of the service— not the prayers, not the scriptures, not the sermon. I don't sing the right words to the hyms that are sung. If they are old hymns known by heart I sing loudly and lustily, but if they are new I hum only the melodies. The words to the rituals are recited from memory, prepared in advance.

Though I cannot say for sure this is true, I suspect I am much better prepared for my ministerial duties without normal eyesight than I would be with it. By this I mean that any professional person who does a significant act over and over becomes lackadaisical about it. Were I normally sighted I would perform a wedding ceremony by reading again the words from the book, as done hundreds of times. I would not prepare myself to do so beforehand because I could trust my eyes to read the appropriate words. Since I cannot rely on that I must prepare myself afresh for each particular service or ceremony.

Most of my advance work, as I've mentioned, is done on cassette tape. With the help of my television reading machine, when I became senior minister I took the prayer book and read all the rituals into the cassette recorder. Now, when I have to perform a baptism, confirmation, wedding, or funeral I simply take out the tape and play it back again and again. I have heard those words over and over so often that I can speak them verbatim from memory. Sometimes I have amused myself by contemplating two future possibilities about this system. In one fantasy, the congregation decides to fire me and hire my tape recorder. At all ceremonial occasions the officiating preacher is the voice from the little black box. I have been automated out of the ministry. In the other fantasy, I get my wires crossed and start spewing out the right words at the wrong occasion, say the wedding ceremony at a baptism. I do sometimes fear that so many words are stuffed into my memory that a sharp blow on my head may set off a torrent of words, drowning bystanders in the rituals of the Christian church (which can happen, I think, with or without tape recorders and memorized ceremonies).

But nothing is that mechanistic. Each of the rituals must be personalized in some way, and of course one preaches a new sermon every week. An elemental fact about the ministry, often ignored by the nonprofessional, is how hard it is to say something different each week to the same group. It is not like perfecting a musical aria and then changing the audience every time one sings. On the contrary, the congregation stays basically the same and the preacher must change. One can write one good sermon or speech and just keep giving it over and over (as I did with The Speech), but it is something else to sing a new aria every time to a constant congregation.

Were you to worship in our congregation on Sunday morning you would hear me preach for twenty or twenty-five minutes. You would recognize it as a sermon: It has prose; it has something to do with scripture and the Christian life; it has anecdotes and illustrative material, similes, metaphors, changes of tone, mood, and meaning. The only possible difference you might notice in my sermon is that it is not read. I could, and sometimes do, stand out from behind the pulpit and just talk to the people in the congregation.

Not having the discipline of a manuscript in front of me, I could be tempted to prattle on and on about anything and everything. That seems to be an occupational hazard—sometimes preaching becomes a kind of sanctified glibness. Before losing my central vision I wrote out my sermons. I knew that eight double-spaced typewritten pages was about twenty minutes of oratory, and the manuscript required such advance preparation that my thought was organized, coherent, and concise. The number of pages disciplined the length. Do that for a few years, and a style and discipline emerge into a set form.

With the loss of eyesight I have learned to use the tape recorder as I used to use the typewriter, and am equally disciplined. Early in the week I speak the sermon into the tape recorder. If I am not satisfied with what I have said I erase the tape and rerecord it until I am satisfied. Eventually twenty minutes or so of sermon is recorded, with biblical references, illustrations, etc., all in audio storage.

That speaking needs to be done in advance of the time it is to be spoken "live." What follows is enough to deter and shame every preacher: I must listen to it over and over again. I hear it maybe fifteen or twenty times before it is preached. The most intensive listening, for several hours, is done just before preaching. To tell you the truth, I am sick of hearing it by the eleven o'clock service! But in that repetition the sequence, key words, and concepts—the whole design and structure—are being etched in my mind.

If you were to watch and listen carefully you could detect two telltale pieces of evidence to identify the process I have followed. The first is appearance: I am direct. I speak straight to people. I look them right in the eyes, even though I cannot see their faces. The second is that my speech pattern is different. I will use words of a series in my sentences and will frequently summarize what I've just finished saying. These are oratorical breathers for me while my brain jumps ahead to what comes next. The pattern is similar to all oratory: A spoken sermon is not literary communication. It is important to rest the audience between points, and it is important to summarize what has just been said. A smart orator does that by calculation; a blind orator does it by necessity.

That is the secret of my preaching style, and I have done it so often that now it has become natural to me. I did not start that way, nor can I honestly say I prefer it that way. But there is something exciting about the adaptability of human beings that is illustrated by this process. If one wants to do something one will find ways to do it, no matter the obstacles.

But How Does He Really Do It?

But public speaking is only a portion of what ministers do. How do I do other aspects of ministry?

I will say, grossly, immodestly, there is nothing any other minister can do that I cannot do. I will add, truthfully, that I may not do them as well as other ministers. But it is greatly reassuring to me and I hope moderately interesting to you that I can perform all the duties of a skilled professional person.

I visit persons in the hospital and also in the parish. When I can do so I walk. I have rediscovered the spiritual resources of walking: Unlike driving a car, one can engage in deep thought while one walks. Some of my best thinking is done on my feet. But it is not always possible to walk. I have had a wonderful relationship with several parishioners who offer their time as chauffeurs. We drive all about conversing as we go, eventually meeting the engagements it is important to keep. I would rather jump into my car and come and go as I please, but there is something good to be said about being disciplined to go when car and driver await you and to go without attention to the hazards of driving. The point is, I do get around.

My secretary is really my professional colleague. She is my eyes in most administrative matters. She reads my mail, keeps my files, organizes my calendar, and gently

shepherds me from one administrative duty to the next.
Between us we have devised helpful little techniques. My
file folders, for instance, are color-coded: green for trustees, red for staff, etc. She prints in large letters my mes-
sages and communications. In that regard, I have no
secrets. If you walked into my office you might see
scrawled across an 8½-by-11-inch sheet of paper the words
"Mrs. Smith wants you to call her." Budgets with their
long columns of figures are the hardest things for me to
master, as I cannot remember numbers as easily as I can
words.

In personal counseling my loss of vision has been a liability and an asset. It is a liability when talking intimately
about a person's deepest hurts and needs and I am unable
to see those little clues trained counselors look for: the
smile or frown on the face, the twinkle or growing tear in
the eye, the telltale demeanor of posture. I really do miss
that. That I can hear better the feeling-tone in a voice is
true but not adequate compensation. Since my loss of normal vision I have a strange inner paradox as I counsel people. I am enormously empathetic when people speak to me
of their hurts, losses, and surprises. I know the feeling: I
have been there, I know it hurts. I know the panic, the despair, the awful struggle to reach for help and healing, and
my hands go out quickly to those who experience these
things. But I am also impatient with the snifflers, com-
plainers, those who think they cannot or will not try to
cope with their altered situations. The combination makes
me gentle but tough. I do not let people feel sorry for
themselves, nor do I let them feel lost and alone.

In pastoral care I think my greatest defect is not recog-
nizing people on sight. I have asked them to tell me who
they are when they greet me after services or pass me in
the hall. Parishioners were good about this at first, but

they have grown weary of telling me who they are, and more positively they have forgotten the need to do that for me. It is bad for church members to have to tell their minister who they are, and I feel it most acutely with children and youth. But I am consistent. I do not recognize my own children if we happen to pass in the halls. In that sense I am unprejudiced: I recognize no one. Maybe in that I have come upon an important democratic value: All people— black, white, young, old, male, female—look the same to me, undifferentiated by the accidents of their appearances, one in their humanity. Strange that sometimes to see a truth clearly one must see it partially.

Is Amy Lowell Right?

The emergence of an affliction invariably sets loose one's introspective and retrospective powers. One looks back beyond the enormous change in one's life to seek patterns of foreshadowing, hints and preparations that may have been operative if one had only the wit to discern them. Are there strange and mysterious ways in which we are prepared in advance for what we encounter? The nineteenth-century poet Amy Lowell wrote a poem entitled "Patterns." In it she wondered as I do whether one could discern in retrospect a design to the events of the present. Her last line was, "Christ! What are patterns for?" In the horrendous agonies of the Civil War, Miss Lowell thought there were no patterns of meaning.

Personally, I take an agnostic stance about the patterns of life one discerns in retrospect. I can set forth some strange and mysterious encounters and developments that, after I lost a portion of my vision, seem to have been foreshadowings or preparations for this change in my life. I could rhapsodize over these earlier events and what they meant were it not also true that I would be engaged in mighty selective recollections. This is the practice of what scholars call revisionist history, i.e., retelling what happened from the special knowledge of what did in fact happen. Yet I can recall from earlier life some unique twists that have helped me adjust to a new reality. As I name these twists I shall let you decide whether these are fore-

shadowings or selective recollections from a wide spec-
trum of experiences. What is unassailable is the fact that
these particular items have become important in reshaping
my life. Amy Lowell may be right, perhaps she is wrong.
No matter, these are the patterns from an earlier life that
helped me contend with my later loss.

Foremost among these "preparations" was my education. With eight years of higher education—four years in a
liberal arts college, three in graduate school, and one
year's internship in Western Springs—I have felt the great
benefits not only of the years but also of their special
fruits: an inquisitive and productive mind that functions in
those ways far beyond the years of academic training.
These fruits have enabled me to function vocationally
through the loss of normal eyesight.

I remember conversing some years ago with a Jewish
friend and asking how it was that many of the intellectual
pillars of the modern world were set by Jewish intellec-
tuals—Einstein, Marx, Freud. Her reply was that Jewish
culture placed high value on the intellect and its development. "Why?" I persisted. "Because," she asserted,
"it is the one thing no one can take away from you." She
was speaking, of course, of the persecutions that have tor-
tured Jewish culture for generations. The barbarians of
any age could knock on one's door and deprive a person of
property, vocation, and family. But they could never con-
fiscate one's education. In an uncertain and insecure world
education became a treasure. I recall her insights now and
they comfort me in their truth. That an above-average
amount of time and money was so spent in my earlier life
was to become a rich benefit later.

I had such a fine education largely by the insistence of
my parents. I was not—and am not—by natural inclina-
tion a scholar. I was never bookish or first in my class. I

was badgered, cajoled, shamed, and driven onward in my schooling. But whatever the carrot in front of my nose, this donkey pressed on through all years of school. My children will be similarly pressured. One knows not what surprises will await them in life. I did not. But I do know that education is the best resource for encountering life's surprises.

I said I was not naturally bookish and that is true. Intellectually curious and well-read—thanks to some fine teachers, I have become so. In retrospect, I see a pattern to my learning that is a bit unusual. When I was in early adolescence the major competitor to my school work was radio. Not the canned music and sentence headlines that characterize today's radio, but old-time network radio with its variety of comedy, drama, action, music, and current events. These programs were an enormous influence on me in early life, which was reinforced in several ways. In the late 1940s my family lived in the Los Angeles area, the home of network radio. I became a pest around the networks, begging for tickets to shows and sneaking into studios just to watch radio productions. Not surprisingly, my first vocational interests were in radio production. I worked part time on several stations and took speech courses in college so I could work on the college station. Had not other interests emerged in my life and had not network radio collapsed with the advent of television, I most likely would have pursued some career in radio broadcasting.

What had an adolescent interest to do with who I am and what I do now? A lot really, when I look retrospectively at the past patterns of my life. Since I cannot read without magnification and even then I read slowly, my ears have become my eyes. Well, not exactly my eyes, but they are certainly an important source of learning and contact with the world. Except for its slowness I really don't mind listening to a book instead of reading it. In addition, the ear enables me to "read" other people's feelings, even their personalities. And it is, as I have explained, how I memorize my sermons and speeches. All in all, that audio turn of mind begun in early life has become a pattern for me in later life.

A third pattern has two roots faint in their origins and not understood in their first appearance, but now in retrospect this pattern seems important. The first root has to do with that audio turn of mind, which took a peculiar twist about two years before my loss of normal eyesight. I went into the cassette tape business.

The idea for the business took shape after reading Otto Friederick's book, *The Decline and Fall of the Saturday Evening Post.* I was editor of *Ministry* at that time, and any book that purported to explain what happened to a premier magazine was must reading. Friederick, the *Post*'s managing editor, contended that, among other reasons, the *Post* collapsed because Curtis Publishing never understood the nature of the business they were in. To Curtis, their business was publishing magazines, so with the profits from their very successful magazines they bought printing presses, paper mills, and timberland for pulp. At the same time they had passed up opportunities to buy the entire Columbia Broadcasting System, to enter the burgeoning textbook field and the enormous paperback industry. The *Post* folded, Friederick wrote, because its publishers thought they were in the printing business not the communications business. Wow, I had thought, how like the situation of my magazine: We are strictly print-oriented. What would our business look like if we were in the communications business? Would we not explore other media for communicating our specialized information?

This was the age of Marshall McLuhan, and all media were undergoing revolutionary upheavals. It was clear to me that we should do a magazine on cassette tape as well as in print. I busied myself assembling the technology of tape-recording, learning the business aspects of advertising, cost accounting, and distribution. I knew nothing of these things, but I was hot on a great idea. I wrote it all up and submitted my Great Idea to our board of directors. In a word, they said no! I was crushed. Had they not read Friederick? No, they had read only our balance sheet, and we had no capital for a new, uncertain venture.

It seemed to me then that two powerful facts had merged: I had a lot of information about the tape business, and a smoldering feeling of rejection. So I did what any Little Red Hen would do when no one else wants to help her with a project: I did it myself. I created my own company, Telepax, and produced and distributed over fifty tapes.

The reason I did that is the second root in this retrospective pattern, viz., I have a very large streak of independence in me. If someone wants me to do something he can get me to do it by telling me it cannot be done. I cannot explain where that defiance comes from. The positive side of this quality is creativity: I am willing to risk new ventures if I think the old ones have not been good enough. The negative side of this quality is that I am slow to accept limits and constraints. That may explain my long uphill fight to accept my loss of eyesight. It certainly explains why my major strategy for rehabilitation was simply to try harder, to work longer, to overcome.

But the curious pattern here is that just as I began to lose my eyesight I was deeply enmeshed in a business venture producing cassette tapes. Within a year the tapes became a great ally in learning to communicate again, but I certainly had not foreseen that when I started the business.

Is Amy Lowell right? Are there patterns that prepare us for the next surprising turn of events? Am I right that in retrospect one practices revisionist tactics and remembers only that which seems pertinent from the present vantage? Either way, the surprise may be that the resources you need for responding to loss are already present in latent form in your own life.

Remembering Some People

My retrospective explorations included not only skills, interests, and attitudes that accrued to me in my earlier life but also some chance encounters with people who I know have affected me mightily.

I suppose that all college alumni have one favorite teacher, perhaps one who not only affected them in college but continued on as a friend and confidant. I had one of those teachers, and the surprising pattern here is that he is blind.

Walter Stromer and I both came to Cornell College in Mount Vernon, Iowa, in the fall of 1953. He came with a Ph.D. in speech, and he was blind. I came as an eighteen-year-old whippersnapper with normal eyesight. It was surprising that we should have become friends, but we did and we are.

Walt is totally blind. Before World War II he had been normally sighted, but in the Battle of the Bulge his optic nerve was severed by shrapnel. He came home a disabled veteran. I don't know the whole of his story, but he told me once that he had not been much of a student until he lost his eyesight. Totally blind, he earned both his master's degree and his doctorate. That had really impressed me then, and it really impresses me now.

He was a teacher of speech, and I had taken his course

so I could mess around the radio station. He took a special interest in me. Even though I was only a freshman, he encouraged me to try out for the debate team. I made it, along with three upperclassmen. I was proud about that, but the best part of that triumph was that I was thrown into a sustained relationship with Walt, who was the coach of the team. We traveled all across the country together, five of us in a car. We ate together, roomed together, even went to the movies together.

Walt was the first blind person I had ever known well. Our relationship went through the several stages that I have come to know in relationships with others. At first I was simply astounded by the novelty of the way he lived. He would show us how he used his Braille card, and how he kept money in different places so he knew what amount he had when he needed to pay a restaurant check. He had marvelous ears. He helped me grow enormously as a public speaker because he heard me so well, knew what to listen for and what it meant, and how to improve what he heard from me. As our relationship matured the novelty disappeared and he became a normal person to me. I paid him the compliment I desire now for myself: I forgot about his blindness.

He did not forget it, of course, just as I now do not forget mine. What he knew so well and what it has taken me so long to learn is that life is more than sight. If you want to be a beggar with a tin cup standing on the corner, you can trade in your freedom and become one. Walt did not. He wanted to contribute to others. His specialty was communication. I learned a lot of speech techniques from him, but what he really communicated was more than oratorical technique. He communicated about life: how to adjust to reality, how to use what remains even though you suffer what has been lost.

Walt Stromer meant a lot to me in those college days. But he means much, much more to me now.

Another man, George Sutherlund, was to me the right man in the right place at the right time. We had had no previous relationship before he came to my home for dinner when I was at the bottom of my elephant mood. I was sure I was and would be good for nothing. As near as we can determine George and I have about the same visual dysfunction. He has had the condition longer than I, and he affected me mightily in several ways.

George was, is, and I presume will continue to be, a research analyst and a partner in a prestigious Chicago brokerage firm. That is a fancy way of saying he has a very responsible, important, demanding job. He helped me a lot just by being a person who despite his loss was highly functional and useful. He has to read thousands of words and keep track of numbers and dollars and output and all that sort of high finance information. It really impressed this depressed elephant that he could do that despite his loss. When one is down it is good to be with someone who has been there before and has returned. It gives hope that there are ways to overcome.

Another helping quality in George was his matter-of-fact attitude. He is not a sentimental romantic like me, but a hard-headed realist. He alone, of all my concerned friends and relatives, did not coddle me. There is a special camaraderie that some in-groups share, a knowledge that pity and coddling will keep you right where you are. Those who have not been there, have not known what it is, have not climbed the barriers, do not share it. It is not that you have no sympathy or pity for one with a similar affliction, but that you possess a knowledge that one can be comfortable wallowing in one's own disappointments. George is not much for wallowing. He thinks the condition is not a tragedy, just a bother. Do you know what he told me at the dinner table, as I described what I could see and could not see? "Yeah, I know—it is kinda like going bald. There is not much you can do about it." Wow! I thought my life was coming unglued, and he told me it was like a minor cosmetic alteration. He understated the consequences, of course, but in a sense he was right: all one's tearful regrets would not alter the facts.

George did one other important thing for me. His own matter-of-fact attitude embodied the fact that his loss of sight was not the central fact of his life. That was important to me at that particular time because my condition had become an obsession. It was all I thought about, talked about, worried about. But life is more than sight. There are other centers of joy and concern. George demonstrated that I need not dwell forever on my loss. Meeting one who had gone ahead of me helped me to acknowledge that truth.

I was helped a lot in my elephant days by a large important group of persons, of whom Alice Jelinek was representative. I had barely known Alice, a fellow member of the Congregational Church, when we met accidentally in front of the post office. She told me who she was and asked how I was coming along. I mumbled something about struggling to cope with my loss, and she responded by telling me of a neighborhood prayer and Bible study group she belonged to, and how they had been praying for me. I believed her. She and this group of distant persons knew I was a human being who had come upon heavy times, and they wanted to focus their prayer energies upon me. I know what that means and have done that for others many times. It may or may not have altered my individual situation, but it did communicate to me that I was not, in fact, an island but was connected in a common fabric with others.

My parents, relatives, colleagues, friends, my church—all were doing prayerful acts for me. It is how religious people care. Sometimes, in some places, religious people should act, should do something. But many more times there is nothing they can or should do. The alternative is to be constant in prayer. Elephants need such prayer. They desperately need to know that the final force in their life is not their own condition or determination. Those they must deal with, and need. But they also need the larger perspective, and that is what prayer groups do. They keep before them the larger dimensions of life and faith.

Another helper in my elephant days was Ken Seim, the pastor of our church. We shared a professional fellowship before, during, and after my struggle with eye disease. But Ken did something for me during the critical days that has been a pastoral example for me. He came to call in my home. That is not spectacular; I have done that thousands of times to my parishioners. Whether it was intentional or not, I cannot say, but he came in the daytime, when I wasn't home. He came to visit with Margie. He was not avoiding or neglecting me, but his spending time with Margie was very important.

I had seen this phenomenon many times myself but had never understood it until that moment. When an affliction strikes a family, the one directly afflicted gets much attention. "How is Bob doing," many asked Margie. But very few had asked Margie, "How are you doing?" In many ways the burden is greater for those not afflicted who care about the one who is. They feel all the pain of the other, plus the awful sense of helplessness. And if they are not careful, they can become satellites to the flickering suns around which they revolve. The afflicted ones need love, care, and prayer, but those riding the wake of affliction are no less desperate. They too need to know that someone cares for them and their alterations.

Ken Seim was especially sensitive to this. He made Margie feel like a person, not a bystander to some Great Event. He listened to her fears about the future for herself and the family. Like a good pastor, he did not tell her what to do or not to worry. He listened to the anxiousness of her heart, and in hearing it, he diminished its power in Margie's soul. Any time one can help affirm the unique integrity and worth of a person and diminish the power of demons in the mind, one has made a significant pastoral call. I try to remember that in my continuing relationships with parishioners.

These, then, are profiles of four persons who helped. They are not the only four, they are representatives of many. There is an old religious cliché—a cliché because it is obvious, old because it has truth to survive: God has no hands, we are his hands.

That is the power of the personal. One human being cannot change what is "permanent, irreparable, and irrevocable" in the life of another. But the afflicted individual functions in an environment, a context, a milieu. He is not an island unto himself but one of an archipelago. Together humans create qualities in the environment which collectively become the field forces of the Divine.

To be cared for may be the most powerful experience in human life. To know that others care for you urges you to care for yourself. To know that you are cared for makes you a participant in the web of life, even when you may not want to participate. To know that you are cared for opens you to the healing, helping power of God which is always there. To know that you are cared for gives you hope.

How Do You Help Another Person?

I really wish I could put into clear, precise prose some surefire directions for helping, like a cake recipe guaranteeing instant success and delight. I cannot, for there are no such words.

To begin on a negative note, it may be that one person can never help another. Such a limitation is contrary to the warp and woof of Christian belief and practice. We are urged from pulpits Sunday after Sunday to follow the example of Jesus, to stop like the Samaritan and bring help to the victims of thievery (whatever its form) on the Jericho road (wherever it is). We are possessed with a strong drive and desire to fix things. We want to make things right or functional or better for those who are afflicted. That is a highly commendable virtue and has helped humanity make great strides.

There is a necessary link that connects people who need help to those with the desire to help. That link is the conviction that the individual must help himself. Sometimes, as in the case of social evils, helping another consists in removing artificial barriers that prevent persons from helping themselves. Sometimes, in the case of illness, it means guiding the healing forces in the body to their own goal of health. Sometimes, in emotional illnesses, it means suppressing the demonic powers in order to liberate the integrative forces for wholeness. But all those kinds of helpful steps are preliminary. They open a door. Whether or not one will pass through the door is another matter.

I can only speak here of my personal experience. I was helped most by those who had themselves walked my path. Henri J. M. Nouwen of the Yale Divinity School speaks in his book, *The Living Reminder*, of wounded healers, those who out of their own pain and struggle give hope and not bitterness to others.

I was helped by those who did not feel sorry for me. I had a strong predilection toward self-pity. Some unknowingly fed that self-pity, keeping me where I was and not helping me move ahead.

I was helped by those who had something to do and did it: Dr. Kaplan's laser beam, Chuck Klindera's carpentry, the church's offer of space.

I was helped by those who listened to me when I wanted to talk. It is surprising how few people really want to listen; many more want to talk. Well-intentioned, they want to tell you what to do, how to feel, what not to worry about, what to believe. These people are rarely wrong but almost always irrelevant. The wounded elephants of this world set their own agenda. There are days when they wish not to speak at all of their situation, others when they want to speak of nothing else. Caring in that context means suppressing one's own agenda until one ascertains the mood in the particular person at the particular time.

I was helped by those with a sense of humor. Humor is a kind of forgiveness, refusing to take one's self and one's circumstances with ultimate seriousness. Laughter has recuperative power. It puts some pleasant distance between one's self and one's circumstances.

I was helped by those who were loyal. Help and healing are not instantaneous, they are a process. Emotions go up and down and round about. Margie and the children stayed with me on these circuitous journeys. Someone you can count on through it all is essential.

Persons who touched my life in these ways were persons who affected a climate, an environment, for that which was already in me to flourish and grow. Surely they were disappointed that I was slow to respond. Surely they were made to feel impotent because they could not right things with a wave of the hand or the shot of a laser. Surely they were troubled by my thanks to them in the form of anger and hostility. I was not myself, but that is the nature of the moment: A wounded elephant is one who is in search of a new self.

Helping people is God's work, but he has no hands. Our hands cannot heal another, but they can participate in a process that liberates the healing power God has placed in each of us.

A Reunion: The Creation of the VIPs

On a cold January of 1974 ten people gathered in my living room. Five of us could not see the faces of the others. The other five, normally sighted, were also afflicted: Their lives had been changed by the loss of sight in someone they cared about. I had not met them before, yet our common visual impairment gave us immediate rapport.

I suggested that we start the evening together by sharing our recent histories, and as I knew this to be threatening I began first. I said I was thirty-nine, the senior minister of a large Protestant church, and legally blind. Through a form of macular degeneration in both eyes I had lost central vision, and only peripheral vision remained. I related what I could and could not do, and how the closed-circuit television system had helped me to read. Immediate interest greeted that news, as none had heard of such a device.

We continued round the circle. Lauretta Vitale introduced herself as a middle-aged former teacher of art. She too had lost central vision, with further complications of cataracts. Peter Pope, a youngish thirty, had had a recent onset of diabetes, causing hemorrhaging in both eyes which allowed him, at best, to see light and dark. He had awakened with it one morning about six months before, and he was a wreck; so was Nancy, his wife. Marian Hupp, a middle-aged housewife who loves to cook and to read, had one good eye only, and her opthalmologist wanted to do laser surgery on that because he feared further complications. Tim Paul was eighteen and a junior in high school, partially sighted since birth due to an oxygen deficiency in his incubator.

So, there we were: five musketeers who had done battle with the enemy. It was clear that eye disease is no respecter of age, class, race, sex, or religion. We were all quite different people, coping and struggling in quite different ways. We had in common a change in our lives caused by the loss of a portion of our sight.

These people were virtually strangers to me, yet I had the nagging feeling I had known them before. That wasn't true. We had only met one another through a friend-of-a-friend sort of thing. We had talked on the phone to arrange for this meeting, but had never . . . Wait a minute! I did know these people. Of course I had seen them before. They were what I used to call "the groupies."

I had often wondered what became of those people. It was clear there were millions of us. I could tell from the depersonalized routine of the medical and technical staffs that we were not the first and only persons they had seen that day, month, or year. Like animals at watering holes we came together for a while and then scattered, never to see one another again. The strange fact of our eye disease is that after it runs its course, does its damage, we disappear. We are not noticeable to each other or to the society. We do not carry white canes, bump into closed doors, or conduct ourselves in ways common to the blind. But never give us a menu to read—we cannot. Never ride in a car with us—we do not see the traffic lights. Never ask us for change—all coins look alike.

That cold January night was turning out to be a reunion. The sad, long faces in the clinics do not just disappear, they slip into their own worlds and try to manage as best they can. It was good to make contact with my estranged brothers and sisters from the waiting rooms of the nation's eye clinics. Even that day as we gathered, hundreds were going to clinics and were trying to explain to their families and friends what had happened and worrying about what to do next.

I had invited this group together for several reasons. Probably because I am a public figure, a minister of a prominent church, I am like a lightning rod, I attract other partially sighted people. I have not hidden the fact of my loss from the congregation, and they tell others of it. Almost everyone knows someone with an eye problem. Word finally gets around about me and a phone contact is made—usually, I might add, with the spouse of the afflicted person. I had thought, why deal with these people on a one-to-one basis? Why not get us together to meet face-to-face?

Further, my Christian convictions have directed me to discover the healing and supportive power of small groups. I was taught the concept in seminary and had experienced it with clergy, with parents, with married couples, all kinds of groups. I believe there is something powerful and redemptive about a group of similar persons who intentionally come together to have their needs met and to meet others' needs. "Support groups" are what we call these today, and why not a support group for partially sighted people?

I was further motivated to convene this group out of my own bitter experience. When my opthalmologist told me my eye condition was "permanent, irreparable, and irrevocable" (dread words!), I had asked where I could turn. The answer was nowhere. Oh sure, there are fine places for the blind. I could be taught to walk with a white cane or a seeing-eye dog, or retrained to do menial work. But I needed none of that. I needed to know what to expect next, what kinds of devices would help me. And mostly, I needed hope that somehow, sometime, my life would come back together in a way that was satisfying to me and useful to others.

Since there was no such group, I asked why not? Why not indeed! If there was no such group, there should be. So the ten of us had gathered to create such a group.

I knew what needed to be done, and for that first night I had planned an agenda I wanted to follow. But my agenda was not to be followed. For a strange thing was happening to these ten people: For the first time in a long time—maybe ever—we were able to talk with others who understood what it was like to be partially sighted. We began immediately exchanging tips about how we functioned. I had always had trouble keeping my socks in fit pairs—brown and black look alike to me. "Easy," said another, "just tie them in knots when you take them off; they go through the wash all right and come back together in your drawer as a pair." Why hadn't I thought of that? Another showed a coin purse that divided all those identical-looking coins into the proper slots. Another woman told how she had put tape on the oven dials so she could set the right temperature without ever seeing the numbers. Very inventive, these people!

The evening was carried by animated conversation, even uproarious laughter. Someone told of how embarrassing it is to find the right bathroom in a darkened restaurant. You mean, that has happened to other people too? I had thought I was the only one who ever made dumb mistakes like that. It is good to know that you are not the only one. It was good to laugh at the recognition of our common sight problems.

At subsequent meetings we were joined by another Bob, also a minister in Chicago; by Ed, the president of a large corporation; Nellie, a resident in a retirement home; Alice, a housewife and golfer. Before the year was up we doubled our numbers, and expect to keep doing that for the foreseeable future.

As we mature as a group we need to develop a form and a structure. We spent a lot of time on names, what we should call ourselves. There are many names for our conditions: partially sighted, visually handicapped, visually afflicted, blinks. We liked none of them as they were negative and restrictive; we are a positive, optimistic group. We want people to know us as functioning human beings, not cripples.

We came upon such a name—an acronym, the VIPs. In our status-conscious society it stands customarily for Very Important People. That was all right with us, that's what we are. But in our case VIP also stands for Visually Inconvenienced People. That is precisely what we are—persons who have difficulty with our eyesight but who are not blind. We may need some help, but not all the helps available to the blind. We are highly functional, creative people, inconvenienced by a loss of some of our eyesight. We like our name, even though we may not like our condition.

The VIPs still need to work on a program and a structure. We have decided there are three primary objectives we should pursue. First, we want to be a support group for partially sighted people and their families. We want to fill that awful gap between the clinics and a return to normal life. We want opthalmologists to refer their clients to us. We all know one or two other people who are as we are, and we want them to tell their friends about us.

It is quite important to include spouses, companions, or

friends in the VIPs. As we don't drive it is almost a necessity to include our chauffeurs. But much more important,
the effects of our eyesight widen into the lives of those
near and dear to us. The companions of partially sighted
people find they have a lot in common, too. For instance,
almost all of us who have been deprived of driving criticize the directional sense and driving habits of others. It
helps to know that we all do that because we are angry at
being deprived of the privilege of driving.

We do restrict participation to the partially sighted. The
totally blind are urged to avail themselves of the social
and philanthropic services directed to them. It is not that
we are snooty, it is that we are distinctive. To be legally
blind, as I am, does not mean that I need the same treatment, training, and therapy as a blinded person.

Our second objective is to disseminate information
about available resources. In other words, we are a clear-
inghouse for information about helps to partially sighted
people. We have "show and tell" nights when members
bring devices we use to lead normal lives. On that first
night in January no one had ever heard of a closed-circuit
television set that magnifies printed words up to three
inches in height so they can be read from a screen with peripheral vision. Light and magnification are the two biggest helps to us, and we have quite a display of lamps and
glasses. What works for one may not work for another,
but it is important to know what is available. Since we are
partially sighted and not blind, there is no central place
where suppliers of helpful merchandise can tell us what is
available. Recent developments, for instance, include cal-
culators that "speak" their numbers instead of just printing
them, a pencil-like scanner that converts printed words
into audio sounds, tape recorders that play fast without
distorting sounds, and the Talking Books of the Library of

Congress on tapes as well as records, which can be procured through local libraries. All these have been demonstrated at recent VIP meetings.

Our third objective is, if you will, a missionary one. We
want to teach our society who we are and what we need.
We have an unspoken credo of interpersonal relations. It
is that each of us may be the only partially sighted person
another knows. How we function or fail will create an image in the other's mind about partially sighted people. We
want it to be good and positive and inspiring.

Further, we want public elements of society to accom-
modate us where possible. For instance, we have prevailed
upon Holiday Inns to publish large-type menus in some of
their dimly lit restaurants. We think all hospitals should
have large signs and room numbers so we can find our
way around. Buses, subways, and other public transport
should have large signs identifying their routes. (Many of
us take expensive cabs because we can tell the driver where
we want to go.)

Those are our three positive objectives, and we have
two negative ones—we will *not* do two things. The first is
that we will not engage in sales of any sort. We know that
when persons are afflicted by eye disease they will clutch
at any straw. Any device offered to them as the salvation
of their loss will be desired even at high prices. So we tell
what is available, but every person has to search it out and
try it out for himself or herself. We urge people never to
purchase any equipment without a protracted test period.
The purchaser needs to be sure that in the long run a particular device and not some other will be of benefit.

The second prohibition is a medical one. We never give
medical advice or opinion, or refer members to certain
doctors. It is true that all of us acquire a great deal of technical information about the eye and its maladies. But a lit-

tle bit of knowledge is a dangerous thing, and we are not competent to diagnose, analyze, or predict what will happen. If someone comes to us and wants to know what laser surgery is like, we will tell of our experiences with the procedure but we will not urge having the surgery. It is against the law to practice medicine without a license, and we want no part of unethical consultation.

As to structure for the VIPs, at this point we are still a very loosely organized group. We have neither charter nor officers. We may come to that, but for now we are sponsored by the members of the First Congregational Church. They provide a place for us to meet in the church and encourage the ministers and secretaries to give leadership and administrative services.

The constituency of the group changes. No one comes to all the gatherings. Basically, we meet once a month for conversation and a program. We have had speakers from various agencies that affect us, doctors and optometrists on the research currently under way, and we have had purely social gatherings, such as Christmas parties.

A recent high point for the VIPs was Tim Paul's graduation from high school. We wanted to have a special party for him and his family, and it was a good celebration. All of us knew from personal experience the enormous effort and patience required for this young man and his family to function fully in a normally sighted world. And I expect we will have another, bigger party in four years when Tim graduates from college.

WHAT GRACEFUL ELEPHANTS BELIEVE

Give It a Name

One of my favorite themes is the power of names.

The process of giving names is important in biblical literature. In Genesis the author goes to great lengths to involve the naming process with that of creation—for instance, "God called the light Day, and the darkness he called Night." Later in the same book when a man named Jacob struggles and prevails, his name is changed to Israel. At the birth of the Christchild it is written, "His name shall be called Immanuel, meaning God with us."

In the oldest of Christian rituals, persons enter the church through baptism. In that ceremony a person, usually a newborn child, is given a name. That name from thenceforth shall be the person's Christian name by which he or she shall be known to man and God.

Why is the naming process important to the Christian religion? Because the giving of a name is not just a label for identification: It is a covenant of ownership, a union of creator with creature, a depiction of some reality greater than meets the eye.

I am writing these words more than five years after that day in the gallery of the United States Senate. By what name should I know and describe my experience? Even now I wonder what it should rightly be called. It has had many names: "macular degeneration," "partial sightedness," "damn shame," even "elephant's ballet." Those have been useful and true names at stops along the way, but in retrospect they do not satisfy the whole process. They are junctures, stages, segments, but looking back over the totality they do not capture the larger scope and sweep of the whole.

Perhaps people, also, should be renamed at funerals. Funeral names could describe the reality that was, baptismal names a potential to be.

The elephant's ballet has been a useful name to tell the story of what happened to me. But now I wish to write of what it meant, and that name will not do. It is too mechanical, too cute. It needs explanation. Meanings are not so personal, subjective—they are accessible to others. The names of experiences that people have given to them become part of the language. Therefore, one must be especially careful what name one gives to an experience, for it will become part of the being of another. That is why biblical authors gave so much attention to naming, and why the name of God, if spoken at all, is said with great reverence and awe.

A good name for my experience is a phrase I learned from a teacher of mine at the University of Chicago. Granger Westberg was the first person in America to have a joint appointment to a medical and a theological faculty. He was the chaplain at Billings Hospital and taught patient care to doctors and clergy. I remember vividly a presentation he made on the stages of grief, subsequently written in a small, helpful book called *Good Grief.*

The phrase that shall name this experience is "response to loss."

Human life is a process of acquisition and relinquishment. We are much better, more skillful, at acquisition than we are at relinquishment. Yet, in the arithmetic of life the two processes must be equal. Everyone loses. We lose life, we lose work, we lose innocence. Because loss is the dark side of life, we cast few illuminating lights upon it. But Christians have some remarkable discoveries to make about loss. They will discover that in his wisdom God has fashioned us to meet loss. We have in our human being a power to encounter the losses of life.

Granger Westberg has advanced a nomenclature that serves well as clues to discover this very special healing gift of God to the human personality. He suggests that there are elements or stages in the response to loss. As each personality and circumstance is unique the process cannot be described with the uniformity of scientific law, but certain general categories seem to be present in one form or another in people who respond to loss. From my unique experience I bear witness that these elements are present, and that when they run their course a healing of sorts occurs.

Westberg says that the first stage in responding to loss is shock and denial. When a loss occurs, the full forces of the human body and spirit recoil and tighten to deny that what is happening is in fact happening. That response is a protective device, like a bumper on a car. The impact is absorbed as gently as possible.

In my case I kept reasserting my good health, my invulnerability to any disease. I presented over and over again my clean medical history. In the first months I would not entertain the thought of any alternatives to my life-style. The double vision was a bother, just a small ripple of deviation from my normal, healthy life. Undoubtedly, the reason all those patients with long, sad faces did not speak much to each other is that each of us was convinced that we were not like the others. This was not really happening to us.

Westberg insists that necessary therapy in this early stage is to gently drive home the fact of what has hap-

pened. It is not a bad dream from which one will soon
awake. The loss is real. That is what Dr. Donald Gass
finally did for me in Miami. Once he said "permanent, irreparable, irrevocable" the healing process was free to
begin. Believe me, I did not like hearing those words, but
as soon as those words were heard with understanding my
change in attitude was initiated.

Emotional outbursts are another stage of grief. Losing
hurts. There is no easy or gentle way to experience loss.
When one loses anything or anyone, there will be a
postsurgical trauma. Our society is not very good at letting human beings express their emotions. Men do not cry,
women ought not be hostile. But pressure builds up inside
a grieving person and it will find a way out. It may be self-
destructive if it does not find expression.

I remember one painful evening in that first year of loss.
I was changing clothes and had put a few coins on the top
of the dresser to put in my pocket. As I looked at the
dresser top I could not see the coins, and instantly a wave
of anger and self-pity engulfed me. I beat my fists on that
dresser and cried buckets of tears. In fact, it was not those
few coins that upset me, they just triggered an outburst
that had been building for months. It had to come out.

Westberg says simply that those emotions must be ex-
pressed. It is probably far easier for the person expressing
those feelings than it is for the loved ones who may receive
harsh abuse in these outbursts, or who are grieving
themselves for the pain of their loved one. Surely their
natural tendency is to assure the person the loss isn't so
bad, that it can be fixed, that it will be all right. But the
power in the outburst is the recognition that it will not be
all right, it cannot be fixed. It is permanent and it hurts
deeply.

Physical distress is the next in Westberg's categories.
The simple fact is that one's loss becomes the center of

one's life; all else is subordinated. In that myopic condition one does not sleep, eat, or play normally. The inat-
tention to these normal pauses and refreshments in life
builds up bodily stress, and one's physical systems may
rebel or collapse at the stressful overload heaped upon
them.

For me, these were minor matters. I did not become ill
or need the care of a physician for any other malady. But I
went to extremes: A head cold, I was sure, was
pneumonia; an upset stomach must be an ulcer. Once one
is convinced of one's physical vulnerability and mortality,
it seems the Final End will encompass one soon.

According to Westberg, just knowing what is likely to
happen is helpful. That may be a helpful insight for doctors to keep in mind when they see their grieving patients.
For grieving persons, not knowing makes us more scared
and uncertain than ever, except that there is some strange
comfort in knowing others do the same thing. Maybe
grieving persons are not as loony as they think they are.

Anger is definitely present in response to loss. I know
there was a simmering hostility beneath the facade of my
placid personality at all times. There still is some there, as
a matter of fact, but with the passage of time its steam
diminishes. In an earlier society grieving people wore
black armbands, as a sign and symbol to all who saw them
that tender loving care was needed. Cross them at your
own risk, they suggested.

Again Westberg has no special corrective therapy except
to know it is likely to happen. This insight, it seems to me,
is best taken by loved ones who often take the brunt of this
anger. Paradoxical as it may be, the one you love the most
is the one upon whom anger is most likely vented. Poor
Margie and the children. As mountain climbers say, they
were assaulted because they were there.

Guilt, Westberg says, is sure to arise in a grieving person, irrespective of moral or personal character. It has to do with that punishment/reward system I mentioned earlier. If one feels blessed in the good of life, it follows that one feels not blessed in the bad of life. Jesus simply said, "The rain falls on the just and the unjust." But that is not good enough for us. We have an intricate system of expectations based on behavior. I went through the quest for discovery of a wrongdoing that could produce such a punishment. It was a futile effort, of course, but I did do it.

Westberg says the guilt phase is positive, in that it means the grieving person recognizes the finality of what has happened. I felt guilty because I realized that a change had occurred and I was powerless to affect it. The grieving person becomes better able to cope when he or she finally believes that a change of consequence has occurred.

When a person is in the depths of pain from a loss, Westberg observes, loneliness becomes a companion. We feel cut off, isolated, removed from the normal activities of life. Others, even intimate loved ones, have returned to their normal ways and life goes on for them, but the aggrieved is stuck with this damnable loss. You go on without me, the loser says.

Loneliness, the sense of isolation, is the positive description of wallowing in self-pity. I did a lot of that. I was deep in this stage of grief when the first call to be senior minister came to me. I refused because I was in the box labeled "keep on the shelf." No one else had ever returned from this valley of shadows. This is where the VIPs can help one another, provided we are not all in this stage simultaneously—in which case we would simply reinforce our feelings of being an outgroup.

This loneliness is manifest in a withdrawal from life. One has been bruised and is not about to be hurt further.

So one pulls up the shell of protection around oneself and presumes to sink to the bottom of the sea while all others go on to frolic in the tides. It is that blue/black mood of despair and defeat.

But then—tentatively, haltingly, mysteriously—the shell opens a crack and one dips maybe only a toe in the water. This is the miracle! We were not made to live lonely, isolated, clammed-up lives. We were made to be involved in life's processes, and that deep, deep urging pulls us out of the shell and back into life.

The return does not occur in the twinkling of an eye; it comes gradually, slowly. An advancement toward life is almost certainly followed by a withdrawal, and one could go on inching upward and outward for years.

In my own analysis, this is where grace came to me, where I found sufficient courage to say to Jim Berry, "I want to try."

The final destination of the stages of grief is not to "get over it" or to "forget it." Rather, it is to readjust to the reality of painful change in one's life. There is nothing desirable or satisfying about the response to loss. No one would intentionally seek it. But if it is true—and it is—that life presents us with gains and losses, acquisitions and relinquishments, then it is good to know that our Creator has not left us destitute in the pain of loss.

Naming an experience of loss, naming the stages through which one passes, is not a miraculous cure that puts us back to where we were before the experience began. But naming the experience is a way of discovering the amazing power and goodness of God in our lives at all times and in all conditions.

The Final Word Is Grace

In the story of the elephant's ballet, the climax of my narrative was the affirmative response to the invitation of the pastoral search committee to be considered for the position of senior minister at First Congregational Church of Western Springs, Illinois.

That affirmative decision symbolized many things. It represented a return to the vocation I had earlier pursued. It was a homecoming, for the third time, to a congregation I already knew and loved and who had helped me pass through a difficult time of life. It represented the closing of a chapter filled with doctors and clinics, of personal uncertainty and determination, unfamiliar upset and dislocations. As that chapter closed another began, a chapter of religious leadership in a religious institution, a reordered work style and family life. But the decision was not just a symbol, though it was that. Something more profound than a vocational choice had happened.

When I wrote the story, I ascribed the change to a new entity. This new entity was made the crux of the change, the enabler of my decision. I called that entity "grace." I owe it to you to say what I think that grace was and is.

In the context of the elephant's ballet I was trying my best to overcome my handicap, and I was doing rather well at it. I was functioning, producing, creating. In the context of the stages of grief, my internal condition was one of loneliness and withdrawal. I was sure that I was and would be a handicapped person. The practice of preaching at the church during the interim and the supportive response of the congregation was one of those testing periods of return to normalcy. But when the invitation came to make it a permanent relationship, I backed off. I could not make a commitment to them because internally I was not ready to make it. In a word, I was stuck.

Stuck is not a pleasant word. It sounds stagnant, an image of wheels spinning but no forward motion. I had never been stuck before, but the older I grow the more I realize that "stuckness" is a powerful fact of life for many. We get stuck in routine, in circumstances, in the mind and in the spirit. All systems are functioning, but motion is absent. It may be that the external terrain is responsible for a person's stuckness. It may be that perseverance is the best tack. But more likely when one is stuck it is caused by internal factors.

I was stuck in a box. It was a box I had fashioned and built for myself. In my case, it was the box of a handicapped person: I, Bob Kemper, had lost an essential of life. I would work very hard to compensate for it, but I would never be what I wanted to be or had hoped to become. Partially sighted people cannot do this, this, or that, I told myself. Yes, I knew there was much I could do and for that I was glad. But because of what I could not do—ever again—I was sure that my options were limited and narrowly restricted.

That box of the handicapped person entrapped not only my vocation, my selfhood, but my spirit as well. The rent for life in that box was my personal freedom: I was paying for life in the box by selling my freedom to sustain it. Esau at least got a mess of pottage for selling his birthright; I got nothing for selling mine but the future of life lived in a box.

Grace, I believe, restores freedom, bursts boxes, and moves us when stuck. How does that happen? How can it be? I am not sure I know. But I believe it does.

Part of its mystical power is perspective. I was stuck in a box without freedom because of where I was looking and what I expected to see. I was looking mostly at things human, not divine. If all one sees or expects to see is humanity—noble humanity, striving humanity, tragic humanity—then surely that is what one will see. And in so seeing, that will be the measure of all things.

Given that source of measure, then, one's worth is in performance. What I did, how well I did it, became the standard of my self-worth. Because of my handicap I felt I could not do well what needed to be done. There is a sense in which that is a true and accurate perception. I cannot do all things as well as I want to. But up to that moment of grace, my whole strategy had been to improve what I did as best I could. And that is not a poor strategy: It did and does serve me reasonably well.

But it is vulnerable at one point: By what authority is performance the measure of self-worth? In a simple, un-sophisticated way, that represents justification by works. I will save myself by doing the best I can. And I still do that up to a point. The point is whether or not that improved performance is where I find self-worth.

It is not. Self-worth comes not from performance but from God. I am worthy not because of what I do but because of what I am. I am a creature of the Creator. Thus, the perspective of grace that comes to "stuck" man, in a box of his own creation, is that one cannot save one's self by performance. That realization is liberating; it gives back freedom. I really am free to screw it all up. I may not do that, I may not want to do that, but by God I am free to do it.

Another part of the mystical power of grace is forgiveness. I was stuck in a box without freedom because I was damned. I had damned myself. I did not put it in these words ever, but the real question thundering in my soul was: Who is responsible here? Who has made this happen? To whom shall I voice my complaint? It is good to have someone to blame. That is why I searched out my ancestors, why I reviewed that past medical history, why I sermonized to doctors about their lack of knowledge concerning rehabilitation. Surely, this whole thing was someone's fault. Mine or theirs. Nail the guilty culprit. Those are the thoughts that keep men stuck in boxes without freedom.

Grace in this sense diminishes the power of the accusative. It is one thing to be unable to fix blame on someone or something. It is quite another not to have to fix blame at all. Not to have to blame one's self or another frees one to meet other dimensions of life.

And another part of the mystical power of grace has to do with time. I was stuck in that box without freedom because I was looking at the whole of my past and the whole of my future. In so searching beyond and before, I could not see the particular moment. I do not know now what the future holds for me. Yes, my loss of vision will make a difference. That cannot be denied. But no one knows the future. You cannot add a cubit to your height and you cannot guarantee tomorrow. No one ever has or ever will. But because I was trying desperately to secure some semblance of certainty for my future, I was stuck, boxed, and unfree. I have no illusions about the future. It could be even bleaker than the past. But the power of that thought is diminished by grace.

Grace, to me, is liberating. It gets me unstuck, out of boxes, and frees me. It does so not by solving riddles or answering questions but by challenging the power of insoluble riddles and unanswerable questions. I have been saved from me.

How that freedom from the box of self remains to be used is the subject of another story. For now this one has ended.